CAMBRIDGE LIBRARY COLLECTION

Books of enduring scholarly value

Literary Studies

This series provides a high-quality selection of early printings of literary works, textual editions, anthologies and literary criticism which are of lasting scholarly interest. Ranging from Old English to Shakespeare to early twentieth-century work from around the world, these books offer a valuable resource for scholars in reception history, textual editing, and literary studies.

The Literary Life of the Late Thomas Pennant

The humorously self-styled 'late' Thomas Pennant (1726–98) published this short auto-biographical survey in 1793. A prominent Welsh naturalist and antiquary, he was known more for his energy and meticulous methodology than for original scientific genius. Yet he helped popularise natural history with beautifully illustrated works such as his *History of Quadrupeds*, the third edition of which is also reissued in this series. Moreover, he is credited with preserving thorough records of antiquities that were later damaged or destroyed. Samuel Johnson, who toured Scotland after Pennant, praised him as 'the best traveller I ever read'. More than a mere travelogue, Pennant's *Literary Life* is full of delightful vignettes – his meeting with the 'wicked wit' Voltaire, his affection for his faithful servant and illustrator Moses Griffith, and his poetic critique of certain hypocritical clergy. The appendices contain several of Pennant's shorter pieces on diverse topics, from anthropology to politics.

T0382603

Cambridge University Press has long been a pioneer in the reissuing of out-of-print titles from its own backlist, producing digital reprints of books that are still sought after by scholars and students but could not be reprinted economically using traditional technology. The Cambridge Library Collection extends this activity to a wider range of books which are still of importance to researchers and professionals, either for the source material they contain, or as landmarks in the history of their academic discipline.

Drawing from the world-renowned collections in the Cambridge University Library and other partner libraries, and guided by the advice of experts in each subject area, Cambridge University Press is using state-of-the-art scanning machines in its own Printing House to capture the content of each book selected for inclusion. The files are processed to give a consistently clear, crisp image, and the books finished to the high quality standard for which the Press is recognised around the world. The latest print-on-demand technology ensures that the books will remain available indefinitely, and that orders for single or multiple copies can quickly be supplied.

The Cambridge Library Collection brings back to life books of enduring scholarly value (including out-of-copyright works originally issued by other publishers) across a wide range of disciplines in the humanities and social sciences and in science and technology.

The Literary Life
of the Late
Thomas Pennant

THOMAS PENNANT

CAMBRIDGE
UNIVERSITY PRESS

CAMBRIDGE
UNIVERSITY PRESS

University Printing House, Cambridge, CB2 8BS, United Kingdom

Published in the United States of America by Cambridge University Press, New York

Cambridge University Press is part of the University of Cambridge.
It furthers the University's mission by disseminating knowledge in the pursuit of
education, learning and research at the highest international levels of excellence.

www.cambridge.org
Information on this title: www.cambridge.org/9781108066365

© in this compilation Cambridge University Press 2013

This edition first published 1793
This digitally printed version 2013

ISBN 978-1-108-06636-5 Paperback

Tho.ˢ Gainsborough, pinx.ᵗ 1776.   Engrav'd by W.ᵐ Ridley.

THOMAS PENNANT Esq.ʳ

AN ÆT. 50.

Publiſh'd according to Act of Parliament March 1.ˢᵗ 1793.

THE

LITERARY LIFE

OF THE LATE

THOMAS PENNANT, Esq.

By HIMSELF.

. . . . cura . . . .
. . . . eadem sequitur tellure repostum.

———————————

LONDON:

SOLD BY BENJAMIN AND JOHN WHITE, FLEET-STREET,
AND ROBERT FAULDER, NEW BOND-STREET.

———————

M.DCC.XCIII.

ADVERTISEMENT.

THE title page announces the termination of my authorial exiſtence, which took place on *March* 1ſt, 1791. Since that period, I have glided through the globe a harmleſs ſprite; have pervaded the continents of *Europe*, *Aſia*, and *Africa*, and deſcribed them with the ſame authenticitý as *Gemelli Careri*, or many other travellers, ideal or real, who are to this day read with avidity, and quoted with faith. My great change is not perceived by mortal eyes. I ſtill haunt the bench of juſtices. I am now active in haſtening levies of our generous *Britons* into the field. However unequal, I ſtill retain the ſame zeal in the ſervices of my country; and twice ſince my departure, have experienced human paſſions, and have grown indignant at injuries offered to my native land; or have incited a vigorous defence againſt the lunatic deſigns of enthuſiaſtic tyranny, or the preſumptuous plans of fanatical atheiſts to ſpread their reign and force their tenets on the contented moral part of their fellow creatures. May I remain poſſeſſed with
the

2

ADVERTISEMENT.

the fame paffions till the great Exorcist lays me for ever. The two laft numbers in the following pages are my poft-exiftent performances. Surviving friends, fmile on the attempts! Surviving enemy, if any I can now have, forgive my errors!

Tu manes ne læde meos.

THOMAS PENNANT.

C O N-

C O N T E N T S.

THE PORTRAIT to be had separate at Mr. *Mazel*'s, N° 7, *Bridges-Street, Covent-Garden.*

THE Bookbinder is desired to place the ruins of FOUNTAIN ABBEY at p. 16.

BE AS A FATHER TO THE FATHERLESS AND INSTEAD OF
A HUSBAND UNTO THEIR MOTHER .

Ecclesiasticus IV. 10 .

The Reverend **JOHN LLOYD** Rector of **CAERWIS**

Born MARCH 25th O:S: 1733. Died MAY 21st 1793 .

The Constant Friend Companion & Assistant to THOMAS PENNANT Esq:

in his Tours in WALES .

Pr: 5sh / JURE X LIBERORUM .

With spear & scarlet now I'm deck'd,
  And sing a jolly song;
But pennyless I must be wreck'd,
  On Limbo's rocks e'er long.

But hope I spy from Bishops kind,
  Like Lighthouse plac'd on high;
If for to change, I heart can find,
  Catches for Psalmody.

My scarlet coat I then will doff,
  For queue a grizzle wear;
The outward man I will put off,
  And prim as Bawd appear.

Away let Oxford Curates trudge,
  And starve with learning great;
For Bishops ne'er can wrongly judge,
  Who've palm'd my empty pate.

I. Sternhold

OF MY

LITERARY LIFE.

VIXI ET QUEM DEDERAT CURSUM FORTUNA PEREGI.

A PRESENT of the ornithology of *Francis Willughby*, efq. made to me, when I was about the age of twelve, by my kinfman the late *John Salifbury*, efq. of *Bachegraig*, in the county of *Flint*, father of the fair and celebrated writer Mrs. *Piozzi*, firft gave me a tafte for that ftudy, and incidentally a love for that of natural hiftory in general, which I have fince purfued with my conftitutional ardor.

A TOUR I made into *Cornwal*, from *Oxford*, in the year 1746 or 1747, gave me a ftrong paffion for minerals and foffils, in which I was greatly encouraged by that able and worthy man, the late reverend doctor *William Borlafe* of *Ludgvan*, who, in the kindeft manner, communicated to me every thing worthy my notice.

THE firft thing of mine which appeared in print was inferted unknown to me; an abftract of a letter I had written to my ever venerated friend and uncle *James Mytton*, efq. on an earth-quake which was felt at *Downing*, *April* the 2d, 1750. This, with feveral fimilar teftimonies, may be feen in the xth volume of the Abridgment of the Philofophical Tranfactions, p. 511.

B   HAVING

HAVING an inclination to the study of antiquities, I was, on *November* the 21st, 1754, elected a fellow of the society of antiquaries.

THIS honor I resigned about the year 1760. I had married a most amiable woman; my circumstances at that time were very narrow, my worthy father being alive, and I vainly thought my happiness would have been permanent, and that I never should have been called again from my retirement to amuse myself in town, or to be of use to the society.

IN the summer of 1754 I visited the hospitable kingdom of *Ireland*, and travelled from *Dublin* to *Balli-Castle*, the *Giants-Causeway*, *Colraine*, the extremity of the county of *Donegal*, *London-Derry*, *Strabone*, *Innis-killen*, *Galway*, *Limerick*, the lake of *Killarney*, *Kinsale*, *Cork*, *Cashel*, *Waterford*, *Kilkenny*, *Dublin*. But such was the conviviality of the country, that my journal proved as *maigre* as my entertainment was *gras*, so it never was a dish fit to be offered to the public.

IN the Philosophical Transactions of 1756, vol. xlix. p. 513, is a trifling paper of mine, on several coralloid bodies, I had collected at *Coal-brook-dale*, in *Shropshire*. It is accompanied by a plate engraven from some drawings by *Watkin Williams*, a person who at that time was an humble companion of my father.

ON *February*, 1757, I received the first and greatest of my literary honors. I value myself the more on its being conferred on me, at the instance of *Linnæus* himself, with whom I had began a correspondence in 1755. I had sent him an account of a recent *concha anomia*, which I found adhering to a sea-plant of the *Norwegian* seas, sent to me by bishop *Pontoppi-*

dan.

dan. Hanc, fays the great naturalift, *recitavi in focietatis regiæ Upfalienfis, publico confeffu,* 1757, *d.* 17 *Februarii, quam collegæ et focii omnes avidiffimè excipiebant et mirati funt; te quoque eodem die membrum præfatæ focietatis unanimo confenfu elegere omnes, et mihi in mandatis dedere hoc tibi fignificandi; probè perfuafi te excepturum hoc eorum officium benevolè, ob amorem quem fers in fcientias et omnia quæ ufui publico inferviant.* My correfpondence continued with this illuftrious perfonage till age and infirmities obliged him to defift. He did me the honor of accepting all my labors publifhed before the year 1774. He fpoke of them in terms too favorable for me to repeat.

About the year 1761 I began my *Britifh Zoology*, which, when completed, confifted of cxxxii plates on imperial paper. They were all engraven by Mr. *Peter Mazel*, now living, and of whofe fkill and integrity I had always occafion to fpeak well. The painter was Mr. *Peter Pallou*, an excellent artift, but too fond of giving gaudy colours to his fubjects. He painted, for my hall, at *Downing*, feveral pictures of birds and animals, attended with fuitable landfcapes. Four were intended to reprefent the climates. The frigid zone, and an *European* fcene of a farm-yard, are particularly well done; all have their merit, but occafion me to lament his conviviality, which affected his circumftances and abridged his days.

FOLIO EDITION OF THE BRITISH ZOOLOGY, 1761.

THE worthy and ingenious *George Edwards*, that admirable ornithologift, at firft conceived a little jealoufy on my attempt: but it very foon fubfided. We became very intimate, and he continued to his dying day ready and earneft to promote all my labors. He prefented me, as a proof of his friendfhip, with numbers of the original drawings from which his etchings had

B 2   been

been formed. Thefe I keep, not only in refpect to his me-mory, but as curious teftimonies of his faithful and elegant pencil.

I dedicated the *Britifh Zoology* to the benefit of the *Welfh* fchool, near *Gray's-inn-lane, London*, and fupported the far greater part of the expence. I loft confiderably by it, notwithftanding feveral gentlemen contributed. My agent was that very honeft man, Mr. *Richard Morris*, of the navy office. His widow was left in narrow circumftances, I therefore permitted her to keep the plates, and make what advantage fhe could of them. I was, at the time of undertaking this work, unexperienced in thefe affairs, and was ill-advifed to publifh on fuch large paper; had it been originally in quarto, the fchool would have been confiderably benefited by it.

JOURNEY TO THE CONTINENT, 1765.

THIS work was for a time left unfinifhed, by reafon of a fhort tour I made to the continent. I left *London* on *February* the 19th, 1765, paffed through *St. Omer, Aire, Arras, Perron*, and acrofs the great foreft to *Chantilli*, and from thence to *Paris*. I made fome ftay at that capital, and was during the time made happy in the company of the celebrated naturalift *Le Comte de Buffon*, with whom I paffed much of the time. He was fatif-fied with my proficiency in natural hiftory, and publickly ac-knowleged his favorable fentiments of my ftudies in the fif-teenth volume of his *Hiftoire Naturelle*. Unfortunately, long before I had any thoughts of enjoying the honor of his ac-quaintance, I had, in my *Britifh Zoology*, made a comparifon between the free-thinking philofopher and our great and re-ligious countryman Mr. *Ray*, much to the advantage of the lat-ter. The fubject was a Mole, really too ridiculous to have been noticed;

LE COMTE DE BUFFON.

noticed; but such was his irritability, that, in the first volume of his *Histoire Naturelle des Oiseaux*, he fell on me most unmercifully, but happily often without reason. He probably relented, for in the following volumes he frequently made use of my authority, which fully atoned for a hasty and misguided fit of passion. I did not wish to quarrel with a gentleman I truly esteemed, yet, unwilling to remain quite passive, in my Index to his admirable works, and the *Planches Enluminées*, I did venture to repel his principal charge, and, *con amore*, to retaliate on my illustrious assailant. Our blows were light, and I hope that neither of us felt any material injury.

I MUST blame the *Comte* for suppressing his acknowlegement of several communications of animals which I sent to him for the illustration of his *Histoire Naturelle*. One was his *Conguar Noir*, Suppl. iii. 223. tab. lxii; my *Jaguar* or *Black Tiger*, Hist. Quadr. 1. N° 190. Another was the drawing of his *Isatis*, Suppl. iii. tab. xvii. which he attributes to good *Peter Collinson*. The third was his *Chacal Adive* of the same work, p. 112. tab. xvi; and my *Barbary* Fox, Hist. Quadr. 1. N° 171, of which I furnished him with the designs. These are no great matters: I lament them only as small defects in a great character.

I took the usual road to *Lyon*, excepting a small digression in *Burgundy*, in compliance with the friendly invitation of the *Comte*, to pass a few days with him in his feat at *Monbard*. His house was built at the foot of a hill crowned with a ruined castle: he had converted the castle-yard into a garden, and fitted up one of the towers into a study. To that place he retired every morning, about seven o'clock, to compose his excellent works, free from all interruption. He continued there

AT MONBARD.

till

till between one and two, when he returned, dined with his family, and gave up the whole remainder of the day to them and
his friends, whom he entertained with the moſt agreeable and
rational converſation.

VOLTAIRE. AT *Ferney*, in the extremity of the ſame province, I viſited
that wicked wit *Voltaire*; he happened to be in good-humour,
and was very entertaining; but, in his attempt to ſpeak *Engliſh*,
ſatisfied us that he was perfect maſter of our oaths and our
curſes.

THE forenoon was not the proper time to viſit *Voltaire*; he
could not bear to have his hours of ſtudy interrupted; this alone
was enough to put him in bad humour, and not without reaſon.
Leſſer people may have the ſame cauſe of complaint, when a
lounger, who has no one thing to do, breaks on their hours of
writing, eſtimates the value of their time by his own, and di-
verts their attention in the moſt pretious hours of the rural
morning.

From *Lyon* I went to *Grenoble* and the *Grand Chartreuſe*, *Cham-
berri*, and *Geneva*, and from thence over the greateſt part of
Swiſſerland. At *Bern* I commenced acquaintance with that
BARON HALLER. excellent man the late baron *Haller*, who, on every occaſion,
ſhewed the utmoſt alacrity to promote my purſuits. At *Zurich*
with the two *Geſners*, the poet and the naturaliſt; the laſt the
deſcendant of the great *Conrad Geſner*.

Ulm and *Augſburg* were the firſt cities I viſited in *Germany*.
Donawert, *Nurenberg*, *Erlang*, *Bamberg*, and *Frankfort* on the
Maine ſucceeded. At the declining city of *Nurenberg* I viſited
DOCTOR TREW. doctor *Trew*, a venerable patron of natural hiſtory. At *Mentz*
I embarked on the *Rhine*, and fell down that magnificent river

as

as low as *Cologne*. From *Duffeldorp* 1 went to *Xanten*, and from thence reached *Holland*; few parts of which I left unvifited.

I efteem my meeting with doctor *Pallas*, at the *Hague*, a momentous affair, for it gave rife to my *Synopfis of Quadrupeds*, and the fecond edition, under the name of the *Hiftory of Quadrupeds*; a work received by the naturalifts of different parts of *Europe* in a manner uncommonly favorable. This and the following year, doctor *Pallas* refided at the *Hague*. From congeniality of difpofition we foon became ftrongly attached. Our converfation rolled chiefly on natural hiftory, and, as we were both enthufiaftic admirers of our great *Ray*, I propofed his undertaking a hiftory of quadrupeds on the fyftem of our illuftrious countryman a little reformed. He affented to my plan, and, on *January* the 18th, 1766, he wrote to me a long letter, in which he fent an outline of his defign, and his refolution to purfue it with all the expedition confiftent with his other engagements. But this work was fated to be accomplifhed by an inferior genius. In the next year he returned to *Berlin*, his native place; his abilities began to be highly celebrated; his fame reached the court of *Peterfburgh*, and the emprefs, not more to her own honor than that of my friend, invited him into her fervice, and in 1768 placed him at the head of one of the philofophical expeditions projected for difcovery in the moft diftant parts of her vaft dominions. This was an expedition worthy of *Pallas*; it began in *June* 1768, and was concluded on the 30th of *July* 1774. It unfolded all his great talents, and eftablifhed his fame equal at left to the greateft philofophers of the age. He was loft to me during that period. On hearing of his return I wrote to him at *Peterfburgh*, and fent to

him

him all the works I had publifhed fince our feparation; he received them with the candor which only great minds poffefs at
the fight of the fuccefsful labors of others.   On *November* the
4th, 1777, I received from him the firft letter of our renewed
correfpondence, which continued feveral years, to my great inftruction.   He fuppreffed nothing that could be of fervice to
the caufe of literature, nor did he defift, till, overpowered with
bufinefs, he dropt all epiftolary duties except thofe which were
official.   To this day he convinces me of his friendfhip by conftant prefents of the productions of his celebrated pen.

Mr. Gronovius.   At *Leyden* I had the pleafure of making a perfonal acquaintance with my worthy correfpondent doctor *Lawrence Theodore
Gronovius*, defcended from a race celebrated for their immenfe
erudition; his own labors will remain lafting proofs of his being an undegenerated fon.

On *February* the 26th, 1767, I was elected Fellow of our
Royal Society.

British Zoo-   Mr. *Benjamin White*, bookfeller, propofed to me the republi-
logy, Second
Edition, 1768.   cation of the *Britifh Zoology*, which was done in 1768, in two
volumes, octavo, illuftrated with xvii plates; he payed me
£.100 for my permiffion, which I immediately vefted in the
Welfh charity fchool.   I may here obferve, that *M. de Murre*,
of *Nurenbergh*, tranflated the folio edition into *German* and *Latin*,
and publifhed it in that fize, with the plates copied and colored
by the ingenious artifts of that city.

In the *May* of this year I met Sir *Jofeph Banks*, then Mr.
Banks, at *Revefby Abby*, his feat in *Lincolnfhire*; during my ftay
I made many obfervations on the zoology of the country, and
muft acknowlege the various obligations I lie under to that
gentleman

gentleman for his liberal communications refulting from the uncommon extent of his travels.

I MAY here mention, that our firft acquaintance commenced on *March* 19th, 1766, when he called on me at my lodgings in *St. James's Street,* and prefented me with that fcarce book *Turner de Avibus,* &c. a gift I retain as a valuable proof of his efteem. An unhappy interruption of our friendfhip once took place, but it recommenced, I truft, to the content of both parties, in a fortunate moment, in *March* 1790.

IN 1769 I added to the *Britifh Zoology* a third volume, in octavo, on the reptiles and fifhes of *Great Britain.* This was illuftrated with xvii plates.

A THIRD VOLUME OF FISHES, &c. 1769.

IN the preceding year fir JOSEPH BANKS communicated to me a new fpecies of *Pinguin,* brought by captain *Macbride* from the *Falkland* iflands. I drew up an account of it, and of all the other fpecies then known, and laid it before the *Royal Society.* They were pleafed to direct that it fhould be publifhed, which was done in this year, in the lviiith volume of the *Philofophical Tranfactions.* It was accompanied by a figure. It is not a good one, the fkin having been too much diftended: but in the fecond edition of my *Genera of Birds* a moft faithful reprefentation is given, taken from the life by doctor *Reinhold Forfter.* I named it *Patagonian,* not only on account of the fize, but becaufe it is very common in the neighborhood of that race of tall men.

My mind was always in a progreffive ftate, it never could ftagnate; this carried me farther than the limits of our ifland, and made me defirous of forming a zoology of fome diftant country, by which I might relieve my pen by the pleafure of

INDIAN ZOOLOGY, 1769.

C

the

the novelty and variety of the fubjects. I was induced to prefer that of *India*, from my acquaintance with *John Gideon Loten*,
efq. who had long been a governor in more than one of the
Dutch iflands in the *Indian* ocean, and with a laudable zeal had
employed feveral moft accurate artifts in delineating, on the
fpot, the birds, and other fubjects of natural hiftory. He offered
to me the ufe of them, in a manner that fhewed his liberal turn.
Twelve plates, in fmall folio, were engraven at the joint expence of fir *Jofeph Banks*, Mr. *Loten*, and myfelf; to which I
added defcriptions and little effays. I forget how the work
ceafed to proceed; but remember that, at my perfuafion, the
plates were beftowed on doctor *John Reinhold Forfter*, together
with three more engraven at my own expence. Thefe he took
with him into *Germany*, faithfully tranflated the letter-prefs into
Latin and *German*, and added a moft ingenious differtation on
the climate, winds, and foil of *India*, and another on the birds of
Paradife and the *Phœnix*, all which he publifhed at *Halle*, in
Saxony, in 1781.

OF MOSES GRIF-
FITH.

IN the fpring of this year I acquired that treafure, *Mofes
Griffith*, born *April* 6th, 1749, at *Trygain-houfe*, in the parifh of
Bryn Groer, in *Llein*, in *Caernarvonfhire*, defcended from very poor
parents, and without any other inftruction than that of reading
and writing. He early took to the ufe of his pencil, and, during
his long fervice with me, has diftinguifhed himfelf as a good and
faithful fervant, and able artift; he can engrave, and he is tolerably fkilled in mufic. He accompanied me in all my journies,
except that of the prefent year. The public may thank him
for numberlefs fcenes and antiquities, which would otherwife
have remained probably for ever concealed.

THIS

THIS year was a very active one with me; I had the hardi-
nefs to venture on a journey to the remoteft part of *North Britain,* a country almoft as little known to its foutern brethren as
Kamtfchatka. I brought home a favorable account of the land.
Whether it will thank me or not I cannot fay, but from the report I made, and fhewing that it might be vifited with fafety,
it has ever fince been *inondée* with fouthern vifitants.

IN the fame year I received a very polite letter from the
reverend *Jo. Erneft Gunner,* bifhop of *Drontheim,* in *Norway,*
informing me that I had been elected member of the Royal Academy of Sciences on *March* the 9th paft; of which fociety that
prelate was prefident.

IN the midft of my reigning purfuits, I never neglected the
company of my convivial friends, or fhunned the fociety of the
gay world. At an affembly in the fpring, the lively converfation of an agreeable Fair gave birth to the

ODE, *occafioned by a Lady profeffing an attachment to* INDIFFERENCE.

FLY, INDIFFERENCE, hated maid!
    Seek *Spitzbergen's* barren fhade:
Where old Winter keeps his court,
There, fit Gueft, do thou refort:
And thy frofty breaft repofe
'Midft congenial ice and fnows.
There refide, infipid maid,
But ne'er infeft my EMMA's head.

    Or elfe feek the Cloifter's pale,
Where reluctant Virgins veil:
In the corner of whofe heart
Earth with Heaven ftill keeps a part:
There thy fulleft influence fhower,
Free poor Grace from Paffion's power.

Give!

Give! give! fond ELOISA reft;
But fhun, oh fhun my EMMA's breaft.

Or on LYCE, wanton maid!
Be thy chilling finger laid.
Quench the frolic beam that flies
From her bright fantaftic eyes.
Teach the fweet Coquet to know
Heart of ice in breaft of fnow:
Give peace to her: Give peace to me:
But leave, oh! leave my EMMA free.

But if thou in grave difguife
Seek'ft to make that Nymph thy prize:
Should that Nymph, deceiv'd by thee,
Liften to thy fophiftry:
Should fhe court thy cold embraces,
And to thee refign her graces;
What, alas! is left for me,
But to fly myfelf to thee.

CHESTER, *March* 1769.

IN 1770 I publifhed ciii additional plates to the three vo-lumes of *Britifh Zoology*, with feveral new defcriptions, befides references to thofe which had been before defcribed; it appeared in an octavo volume of 96 pages, in which is included a lift of *European* birds extra *Britannic*.

IN 1771 I printed, at *Chefter*, my *Synopfis of Quadrupeds*, in one volume, octavo, with xxxi plates.

ON *May* the 11th, 1771, I was honored by the univerfity of *Oxford* with the degree of doctor of laws, conferred on me in full convocation. I was prefented (in the abfence of the public orator) by the reverend Mr. *Fofter*, who made a moft flattering fpeech on the occafion.

IN

In *September*, of the fame year, I took a journey to *London*, to fee fir *Jofeph Banks* and doctor *Solander*, on their arrival from their circumnavigation. In my return I vifited *Robert Berkeley*, efq. of *Spetchly*, near *Worcefter*, to indulge my curiofity with feeing and examining Mr: *Faulkner*, an aged j fuit, who had paffed thirty-eight years in *Patagonia*; his account fatisfied me of the exiftence of the tall race of mankind. In the appendix to this work, I have given all I could collect refpecting that muchdoubted people.

FATHER FAULK-NER, A JESUIT.

About this time I gave to the public my *Tour in Scotland*, in one volume octavo, containing xviii plates. A candid account of that country was fuch a novelty, that the impreffion was inftantly bought up; and in the next year another was printed, and as foon fold.

TOUR IN SCOT-LAND IN TWO EDITIONS.

In this tour, as in all the fucceeding, I labored earneftly to conciliate the affections of the two nations, fo wickedly and ftudioufly fet at variance by evil-defigning people. I received feveral very flattering letters on the occafion. An extract of one, from that refpectable nobleman, the late earl of *Kinnoull*, dated *February* the 27th, 1772, may ferve *inftar omnium*.

" I perused your book, for which I return my hearty thanks,
" with the greateft pleafure; every reader muft admire the
" goodnefs of the author's heart; the inhabitants of this part of
" the united kingdoms fhould exprefs the warmeft gratitude
" for your candid reprefentation of them and their country.
" This, unlefs my countrymen wifh to forfeit the favorable opi-
" nion you entertain and endeavor to imprefs upon the minds
" of their fellow fubjects, muft procure you their beft thanks.

* " It

" It would be a worfe reflection upon us, than any that has
" fallen from the moft envenomed pen, if the writer of that
" account did not meet with the moft grateful acknowlege-
" ment."

DOCTOR FOR-
STER'S AMERI-
CAN CATA-
LOGUE.
IN this year doctor *Forſter* publifhed a catalogue of the animals of *North America.* I had begun the work, by a lift of the
quadrupeds, birds and fifhes. Doctor *Forſter* added all the reft:
and afterwards, in a new edition, favored the world with a moft
comprehenfive *Flora* of that vaft country, with a catalogue
of infects, and the directions for preferving natural curiofities.
My part in this work is of fo little merit that it need not be
boafted of. I only lay clame to my proper right.

IT was in this year that I laid before the *Royal Society* an account of two new fpecies of Tortoifes. The one a frefh-water
fpecies, known in *North America* by the name of the *Soft-ſhelled
Tortoiſe.* It is attended by a very accurate hiftory of its manners, and two fine figures, communicated to me by the worthy
doctor *Garden,* of *Charleſtown, South Caroline.* My paper was
publifhed in vol. lxi. of the Tranſactions, attended by a plate.
This is the *Teſtudo ferox* of *Gmelin, Lin.* iii. 1039. and *Le Molle* of
La Cepede, i. 13. tab. vii.

THE other is a fmall and new fpecies, which I name the tu-
berculated. *Le Comte de la Cepede* and Mr. *Gmelin* err in making it the young of the *Coriaceous Tortoiſe, Br. Zool.* iii. N° 1.
Le Luthe of *de la Cepede,* i. 115. tab. iii. and *T. Coriacea* of
Gmelin, 1036. B. *T. tuberculata.*

THIS year another little poetical piece was produced, by the
accident

accident of a lady being chosen, on the same day, patroness of a Book-society and Hunting-meeting.

> THE sons of the Chace, and of Knowlege convene,
> Each to fix on a patroness fit;
> 'Midst the deities one had DIANA, chast Queen!
> The other the Goddess of Wit.
>
> But on earth, where to find Representatives pat,
> For a while did much puzzle each wight;
> One Nymph wanting this, and one wanting that,
> Disqualified each clamant quite.
>
> Then says CHIRON, the case I have hit to a hair,
> Since in numbers none equal I find,
> I have thought of one Nymph, not VENUS more fair,
> In whom is each Goddess combin'd.
>
> Over wit then in heaven let MINERVA preside,
> Soft discretion DIANA may boast.
> Amidst mortals I am sure none our choice can deride,
> When we name bright ELIZA our toast.

CHESTER, *Sept.* 20, 1771.

ON *May* the 18th, 1772, I began the longest of my journies in our island. In this year was performed my second tour in *Scotland*, and my voyage to the *Hebrides*: my success was equal to my hopes; I pointed out every thing I thought would be of service to the country; it was rouzed to look into its advantages; societies have been formed for the improvements of the fisheries, and for founding of towns in proper places; to all which, I sincerely wish the most happy event; vast sums will be flung away; but incidentally numbers will be benefited, and the passion of patriots tickled. I confess that my own vanity was

x

greatly

greatly gratified by the compliments paid to me in every cor-
porated town; *Edinburgh* itſelf preſented me with its freedom,
and I returned rich in civic honors.

I PUBLISHED the octavo edition of *Genera of Birds* in 1773,
and gave with it an explanatory plate.

THIS likewiſe was a year of great activity. I rode (for almoſt
all my tours were on horſeback) to Mr. *Graham's* of *Netherby,*
beyond *Carliſle,* through thoſe parts of *Lancaſhire, Weſtmoreland,*
and *Cumberland,* which I had not before ſeen. I viſited *Sefton,*
Ormſkirk, Blackburne, and *Clithero,* in *Lancaſhire; Malham Coves,*
Settle, and *Ingleborough,* in *Yorkſhire; Kirkby Lonſdale, Kirkby*
Stephen, and *Orton,* in *Weſtmoreland;* and all the counteſs of
Cumberland's caſtles in that county; *Naworth, Corbie,* and *Beu-*
caſtle, in *Cumberland.* In my way I ſkirted the weſtern ſide of
Yorkſhire; I paſſed ſome hours with the reverend doctor *Burn*
at *Orton,* in *Weſtmoreland,* a moſt uſeful and worthy cha-
racter.

FROM *Netherby* I croſſed *Alſton Moor* into the biſhoprick of
Durham, made ſome ſtay with its prelate, doctor *John Egerton,*
and entered *Yorkſhire* after croſing the *Tees* at *Barnard Caſtle.*
From thence I viſited *Rokeſby* houſe; *Catterick* bridge; the ſingular circular entrenchments attributed to the *Danes:* the pictureſque *Hackfall,* and the venerable remains of *Fountaine's* abby.
The laſt attracted my attention ſo much that I reviſited them
in *May* 1777, and each time they gave full employ to the pencil of *Moſes Griffith.* He etched two of his drawings: I here
give one of the plates, as a ſpecimen of his extenſive
genius.

FROM thence I croſſed to *Boroughbridge* and *Knareſborough.*
                                                                        From

Moses Griffith, del: et sculp.

Part of the inside
of the CHURCH of FOUNTAINS ABBY.

From *Harrogate* I vifited the wonderful *lufufes* of *Bramham* crags, and caufed great numbers of drawings to be made of the moft ftriking pieces.

From *Harrogate* I rode to *York*, where *Mofes Griffith* was by no means idle. Among many other drawings, I caufed him, out of veneration to the tafte of Mr. *Gray*, to make a fecond drawing * of the chapel, fo much admired by that elegant genius. From *York* I rode the great diagonal of the county to *Spurnhead*. Near *Hull*, payed a fecond time my refpects to my friend *William Conftable*, efq. of *Burton Conftable*, a gentleman the moft happy in a liberal and munificent turn of mind of any one I know. I kept along the *Humber*, and from its banks went to *Howden*, *Pontefract*, *Doncafter*, and *Kiveton*; vifited *Work-fop*, *Welbeck*, the antient houfe of *Hardwick*, *Bolfover Caftle*, *Derby*, *Dovedale*, *Buxton*, *Leek*; and proceeded by *Congleton* and *Chefter* to my own houfe. I kept a journal of the whole I mention, as well as numberlefs places which I omit. In every tour I made I kept a regular journal, all which are placed apart in my library; thefe I wifh never to be made public, as they may contain inaccuracies, either from hafte or mifinformation: yet, as they contain many defcriptions of buildings, and accounts of places in the ftate they were at the time they were made, they ought not totally to be neglected.

Mofes Griffiths made numbers of drawings: my ingenious friend Mr. *Grofe* honored me with ufing feveral for his fine work of the Antiquities of *England*; and I believe Mr. *Hut-*

WILLIAM CON-
STABLE, ESQ.

MR. HUTCHIN
SON.

* See Memoirs of his Life, &c. p. 294, fecond edition.

D   *chinfon,*

chinſon, cf *Bernard Caſtle*, will do the ſame in his hiſtory of *Durham*.

I COMMENCED a friendſhip with that gentleman in this jour-ney, in a moſt ſingular manner: I was mounted on the famous ſtones in the church-yard of *Penrith*, to take a nearer view of them, and ſee whether the drawing I had procured, done by the rev. doctor *Tod*, had the leſt foundation in truth. Thus en-gaged, a perſon of good appearance, looking up at me, obſerved " what fine work Mr. *Pennant* had made with thoſe ſtones !" I ſaw he had got into a horrible ſcrape; ſo, unwilling to make bad worſe, deſcended, laid hold of his button, and told him, " I am the man !" After his confuſion was over, I made a ſhort de-fence, ſhook him by the hand, and we became from that moment faſt friends.

THE ſubject of part of this journey will be found among my poſthumous works, fairly tranſcribed, neatly bound in vellum, and richly illuſtrated with drawings by *Moſes Griffith*, and with prints. This will take in the ſpace from *Downing* to *Orford*, the ſeat of my worthy and venerable friend the late *John Blackburne*, eſq. From thence to *Knowſly*, *Sephton*, *Ormſkirk*, *Latham*, and (croſſing the country) to *Blackborn*, *Whalley-abby*, *Ribcheſter*, *Mitton*, *Waddington-hall*, and *Clithero*, moſt of them in the county of *Lancaſhire*. In that of *York*, I viſited *Sally-abby*, *Bolton-hall*, *Malham Coves*, *Settle*, *Giggleſwick*, and *Ingleton*.

I THEN croſſed the *Lune* to *Kirkby Lonſdale*, and viſited all the parts of *Weſtmoreland* and *Cumberland*, omitted in my printed tours of 1769 and 1772 : and finally I finiſhed this M.S. vo-lume at *Alſton*, near the borders of *Durham*. For a more full

I   account

account of my various *poſthuma* I refer the reader to the latter pages of this book.

In this year I kept a regular journal of the road between my houſe and *London,* and did the ſame on my return, digreſſing to the right or to the left, as the places which merit notice happened to lie.

I began the account of this excurſion with ſaying, that almoſt all my tours were performed on horſeback; to that, and to the perfect eaſe of mind I enjoyed in theſe pleaſing journies, I owe my *viridis ſeneċtus*; I ſtill retain, as far as poſſible, the ſame ſpecies of removal from place to place. I conſider the abſolute reſignation of one's perſon to the luxury of a carriage, to forebode a very ſhort interval between that, and the vehicle which is to convey us to our laſt ſtage.

In 1774 I publiſhed a third edition of my *Tour in Scotland,* 1769, in quarto, with the xxi new plates; but, to accommodate the purchaſers of the firſt edition, I republiſhed, with letter-preſs of the octavo ſize, all thoſe plates.

1774.
THIRD EDITION
OF MY FIRST
TOUR IN SCOT-
LAND.

In this edition appeared a ſmall poem of mine, in reply to a moſt amiable dignitary, now high on the bench of biſhops, who had written to me, half-jeſt, half-earneſt, on an invidious compariſon I had made between the *Engliſh* and *Scotch* clergy. I thought it beſt to make my defence in rhyme, ſo ſent him the lines in p. 173 of that edition, and all was well again; my coloring of the portraits I gave is certainly high, but the likeneſſes are confeſſed by all who have ſeen the originals. The reader need not be informed, that the ſeven firſt lines are borrowed from the inimitable author of the *New Bath Guide.*

D 2　　　　　'FRIEND.

'FRIEND.

' YOU, you in fiery purgat'ry muſt ſtay
' Till gall, and ink, and dirt of ſcribbling day
' In purifying flames are purg'd away.

'TRAVELLER.

' O truſt me, dear D * * *, I ne'er would offend
' One pious divine, one virtuous friend:
' From nature alone are my charaƈters drawn,
' From little *Bob Jerom* to biſhops in lawn.'
O truſt me, dear friend, I never did think on
The holies who dwell near th' o'erlooker of *Lincoln.*
Not a prelate or prieſt did e'er haunt my ſlumber,
Who inſtruƈtively teach betwixt *Tweeda* and *Humber*;
Nor in ſouth, eaſt, or weſt do I ſtigmatiſe any
Who ſtick to their texts, and thoſe are the MANY.
But when croſſing and joſtling come queer men of G-d,
In ruſty brown coats, and waiſtcoats of plaid,
With greaſy cropt hair, and hats cut to the quick,
Tight white leathern breeches, and truncheon-like ſtick;
Clear of all that is ſacred from bowſprit to poop, ſir;
Who prophane like a pagan, and ſwear like a trooper;
Who ſhine in the cock-pit, on turf and in ſtable,
And are the prime bucks and arch wags of each table;
Who, if they e'er deign to thump drum eccleſiaſtic,
Spout new-fangled doƈtrine, enough to make man ſick;
And lay down as goſpel, but not from their Bibles,
That good-natur'd vices are nothing but foibles;
And vice are refining, till vice is no more,
From taking a bottle to taking a * * * * *.

Then

Then if in thefe days fuch apoftates appear,
(For fuch, I am told, are found there and here)
O pardon, dear friend, a well-meaning zeal,
Too unguardedly telling the fcandal I feel:
It touches not you, let the galled jades winch,
Sound in morals and doctrine you never will flinch.
O friend of paft youth, let me think of the fable
Oft told with chafte mirth at your innocent table,
When, inftructively kind, wifdom's rules you run o'er,
Reluctant I leave you, infatiate for more;
So, bleft be the day that my joys will reftore!

I AM a fincere well-wifher to the pure form of worfhip of the church of *England*, and am highly fcandalized if I fee any thing wrong in the conduct of our hierarchy. Now and then complaint has been made againft the unguarded admiffion of perfons of the moft difcordant profeffions into the facred pale, who, urged by no other call than that of poverty, do not prove either ornamental or ufeful in their new character. To check the progrefs of a practice injurious to the church, and highly fo to thofe who had fpent their fortune in a courfe of education for the due difcharge of their duties, I fent a farcaftic, but falutary print, into the world: at which even bifhops themfelves have deigned to fmile.

IN the fame year I publifhed my journey into *Scotland*, and my voyage to the *Hebrides*, in one volume quarto, with xliv plates. In this work the beautiful views of the *Bafaltic Staffa* appeared. I had the bad fortune to be denied approach to that fingular ifland; but, by the liberal communication of Sir

VOYAGE TO THE HEBRIDES PUBLISHED.

§   *Jofeph*

Joseph Banks, who touched there the fame year, in his way to *Iceland*, the lofs to the public was happily fupplied.

VOYAGE TO THE
ISLE OF MAN.

In this year I vifited the *Ifle of Man*, in company with the reverend doctor *Lort*, captain *Grofe*, *Paul Panton*, efq. junior, of *Plas Gwyn*, in the ifland of *Anglefey*, and the reverend *Hugh Davies*, at this time rector of *Aber* in *Caernarvonfhire*, whofe company gave additional pleafure to the tour. I kept a journal, and was favored with ample materials from the gentlemen of the ifland, moft of which were unaccountably loft about a year after, and my defign of giving an account of that ifland to the public was fruftrated.

I SHOULD accufe myfelf of a very undue neglect, if I did not acknowlege the various fervices I received from the friendfhip of Mr. *Davies*, at different times, fince the beginning of our acquaintance. I will in particular mention thofe which refulted from his great knowledge in botany. To him I owe the account of our *Snowdonian* plants; to him I lie under the obligation for undertaking, in *June* 1775, at my requeft, another voyage to the *Ifle of Man*, to take a fecond review of its vegetable productions. By his labors a *Flora* of the ifland is rendered as complete as poffible to be effected by a fingle perfon, at one feafon of the year. The number of plants he obferved amounted to about five hundred and fifty.

A TOUR, 1774,
INTO NOR-
THAMPTON-
SHIRE.

In the fpring of 1774, on my return from my annual vifit to *London*, I took the *Northamptonfhire* road, paffed by *Baldock*, *Eaton*, *St. Neots*, *Kimbolton*, *Thraipfton*, *Draiton-boufe*, *Luffwick* and its fine tombs, *Broughton-boufe*, and the monuments at *Warkton*, *Leicefter*, *Afhby de la Zouch*, *Bradford-ball*, celebrated in

Grammont's

Grammont's Memoirs, through *Burton on Trent*, and by *Caverfal Caftle* to my own houfe.

On *Auguft* the 26th I brought my fon *David* to *Hackney* fchool, and placed him under the care of Mr. *Newcome*. In my way I faw *Whitchurch, Cumbermere, Newport, Tong Caftle*, and the tombs in the church, *Ombrefley, Weftwood-houfe, Henlip, Crome*, the two *Malvernes*, and *Tewkefbury*; and, after paffing a few days at my refpected friend's, the then bifhop of *St. David's*, at *Forthampton*, proceeded and difcharged my duty at *Hackney* by the way of *Gloucefter* and *Cheltenham*.

NEWPORT, TONG, OMBRESLEY, MALVERNE, AND TEWKESBURY.

I NEVER loft an opportunity of enlarging my knowlege of topography: on my return I had the honor of paffing fome days with her grace the late dutchefs dowager of *Portland*, at her feat at *Bulftrode*, and vifited from thence *Windfor* and *Eaton*; I alfo one morning faw the great houfe of *Stoke Pogeis*, then the feat of Mr. *Penn*; it had gone through many great hands. In the reign of *Edward* III. it belonged to *John de Molin*, a potent baron, in right of his wife, daughter of *Robert Pogeis*. From *Bulftrode*, I took the common road to *Worcefter*, paffed a day or two, as ufual, at *Beverey*, with my old and conftant friend the reverend doctor *Nafh*, author of the Antiquities of *Worcefter-fhire*: from his houfe went by *Stourport* and *Bewdley* to *Bridge-north*, and from thence through *Newport* to *Downing*.

BULSTRODE, WINDSOR, STOKE POGEIS, BEWD-LEY.

In 1775 I publifhed my third and laft volume of my *Tour in Scotland*, 1772, which took in the country from my landing at *Armaddie*, on the conclufion of my voyage to the *Hebrides*, to my return into *Flintfhire*. This was illuftrated with xlvii plates.

THIRD VOLUME OF MY TOUR IN SCOTLAND PUB-LISHED 1775.

THESE tours were tranflated into *German*, and abridged in *French*,

French, in the *Nouveau Recueil de Voyages au Nord, &c.* 3 tom. quarto, *Geneve*, 1785; they were likewife reprinted at *Dublin*, in octavo fize.

TOUR IN 1776.   IN my road, in 1776, from *London*, I vifited *Banbury*, *Wroxtön-hall* the feat of lord *Guildford*, *Buckingham*, *Edge-hill*, *Charlcot* the feat of the *Lucies*, *Warwick* and *Kenelworth*, and paffed through *Coventry*, *Atherfton*, and *Tamworth* to *Downing*. At *Buckingham* I narrowly efcaped a death fuited to an antiquary; I vifited the old church at 8 o'clock in the morning of *March* the 26th. It fell before 6 in the afternoon, and I efcaped being buried in its ruins.

ON *July* the 14th I took the route of *Oulton-hall*, *Winnington*, and *Durham* in *Chefhire*, vifited *Manchefter*, *Buxton*, *Bakewell*, *Haddon-hall*, *Matlock*, *Nottingham*, *Southwell*, *Newark*, and *Lin-coln*. Near *Horn-caftle* I entered the *Pais-bas* of *Great Britain*. I vifited *Taterfale* and *Bofton*, *Spalding*, *Crowland-abby*, *Stamford*, *Burleigh-houfe*, *Caftor* and *Peterborough*, *Whittlefea-marfh* and *Ely*, *Newmarket*, *St. Edmundfbury*, the reverend Mr. *Afhby* at *Barrow*, *Cambridge*, *Ware*, and *Waltham-abby*; paffed a day with Mr. *Gough* at *Enfield*, and concluded my tour in the capital.

IN this journey *Mofes Griffith* made fome of his moft beautiful drawings in the line of antiquity: of feveral of the moft elegant parts of the *gothic* architecture in the magnificent cathedral at *Lincoln*; and alfo a few of the groffer figures in the *Saxon* remains of the weft front; and at *Southwell* he drew the exquifite interior of the matchlefs chapter, one of the lighteft and moft elegant productions of the *gothic* chizel which we can boaft of. I wifh my time would permit me to make a cata-

logue

logue of the performances of *Moses Griffith*. I never should
deny copies of them to any gentleman who would. make a dig-
nified use of them.

In this year *Peter Brown*, a *Dane* by birth, and a very neat
limner, published his illuftrations of natural history in large
quarto, with L plates. At my recommendation, Mr. *Loten*
lent to him the greateft part of the drawings to be engraven,
being of birds painted in *India*. I patronized *Brown*, drew up
the greateft part of the defcriptions for him, but had not the
left concern in the preface.

BROWN'S ILLUS-
TRATION OF
NATURAL HIS-
TORY.

In 1776 Mr. *White* published a new edition of the three volumes of the *British Zoology*, in quarto, and in octavo, and inferted in them the ciii additional plates published in 1770.

In the fpring of the year 1777 I made an excurfion from
town to *Canterbury*, along the poft road, and digreffed from
Canterbury to *Sandwich*, and from thence to *Deal*, and by *St.
Margaret*'s church and *Cliff* to *Dover*. In this tour I had the
happinefs of making acquaintance with Mr. *Latham* of *Dartford*, Mr. *Jacobs* of *Feverfham*, and Mr. *Boys* of *Sandwich*; all
perfons of diftinguifhed merit in the ftudy of natural hiftory
and antiquities.

1777.
TOUR IN KENT.

In that year I published a fourth volume of the *British Zoology*,
which contained the *Vermes*, the *Cruftaceous*, and *Teftaceous* animals of our country; this was published in quarto and octavo,
and illuftrated with xciii plates.

To this volume I prefixed a moft merited eulogy on my
refpected friend *Benjamin Stillingfleet*, efq. who died *Dec.* 15th,
1771, at his lodgings in *Piccadilly*, aged 71. His public and
private character might demand this tribute: but the many

E   perfonal

perſonal acts of friendſhip I received from that moſt amiable man, was an irreſiſtible incitement to me to erect this ſmall, but very inadequate, monument of gratitude.

Tour in Wales.
AFTER ſeveral journies over the ſix counties of *North Wales*, in which I collected ample materials for their hiſtory, I flung them in the form of a tour, and publiſhed the firſt volume in quarto, with xxvi plates, in 1778.

1778.

1781.
Second Volume.
IN 1781 the firſt part of the ſecond volume of the ſame tour appeared, under the title of, *A Journey to Snowdon*, with xi plates, a frontiſpiece, and 2 vignets. The ſecond part ſoon followed, with xv plates, and a large appendix, which completed the work. In all my journies through *Wales*, I was attended by my friend the reverend *John Lloyd*, a native of *Llanarmon*, and rector of *Caerwis:* to his great ſkill in the language and antiquities of our country I own myſelf much indebted; for without his aſſiſtance, many things might have eſcaped me, and many errors crept into my labors.

Moses Grif-
fith's Supple-
mental Plates.
Moſes Griffith engraved a Supplement of x plates, to which I added a litttle preface, and a few explanatory pages. Beſides theſe proofs of his ingenuity, he etched ſeveral other (private plates) ſuch as, about a dozen *North American* birds, two beautiful parts of *Fountains-abby*, and a few other things.

History of Qua-
drupeds.
IN this year I alſo publiſhed a new edition of my *Synopſis of Quadrupeds*, in two volumes, quarto, with lii plates, including the xxxi from the Synopſis, which received conſiderable improvements and corrections from the correſpondence of my friend the illuſtrious *Pallas*, who beſtowed a long ſeries of letters on this alone; this he performed, as it was a favorite work of his, and by accident transferred from his, to my inferior pen.

To

To Mr. *Zimmerman* I was greatly indebted for several important improvements, from his able performance the *Zoologia Geographica*, as well as great information from his frequent letters. It is unbecoming in me to express the partiality which that eminant writer, and other of my foreign friends, have shewn towards me: if the reader has the curiosity to learn their opinion of me, he may consult Mr. ZIMMERMAN's *Zoologia Geographica*, p. 286. The rev. Mr. Cox, in vol. II. p. 440, 441, of his travels, quarto edition, hath recorded the compliment paid to me by LINNÆUS; and PALLAS, in p. 376 of his *Nova Species Quadrupedum*, hath dealt out his praise with much too liberal a hand.

The liberties which the country gentlemen, in the character of deputy-lieutenants, and militia-officers, now and then took with their fellow subjects, urged me strongly this year to publish *Free Thoughts on the Militia Laws*. *FREE THOUGHTS ON THE MILITIA LAWS.*

ON *Feb.* the 3d, 1781, I was elected honorary member of the Society of Antiquaries at *Edinburgh*.

IN the *Philosophical Transactions* of 1781 was published my history, and natural history, of the *Turky*; it had been doubted whether this was not a bird of the old world; but I flatter myself that I have made it apparent that it is peculiar to *America*, and was unknown before the discovery of that continent. My respected friend, Mr. *Barrington*, had taken the other side of the question; but this was not published by me polemically, or in any wise inimical to so excellent a character. *OF THE TURKY.*

To this paper is annexed an engraving of a singular *Lusus*, the toe and claw of some rapacious bird growing on the thigh of a *Turky*, bred in my poultry court.

At the requeſt of Sir *Joſeph Banks* I drew up an account of the ſeveral earthquakes I had felt in *Flintſhire*; and remarked they were never felt at the bottom of lead mines, or coal pits, in our country. This paper was publiſhed, in the year 1781, in volume lxxi of the *Philoſophical Tranſactions*.

1782.
JOURNEY TO
LONDON.

In 1782 I publiſhed my journey from *Cheſter* to *London*; this was formed from journals made at different times in my way to town. I frequently made a conſiderable ſtay at ſeveral places, to give this book all the fulneſs and accuracy in my power. This was republiſhed in *Dublin*, in 1783, in an octavo form.

1783.

On *June* the 5th, 1783, I was honored by my election into the *Societas Phyſiographica* at *Lund*, in *Sweden*; a favor I probably owed to my learned friend, profeſſor *Retzius*.

In the ſame month and year I made a ſhort elopement to meet the reverend doctor *Naſh*, Mrs. and Miſs *Naſh*, at *Shrewſbury*, in order to make a partial voyage down the *Severn*. My ſon met us from *Oxford*, and we took boat at *Atcham-bridge*. About four miles diſtant from *Salop*, we were highly amuſed with the pictureſque ſcenes, eſpecially thoſe from *Buildas* to *Ombreſley*. We landed oppoſite to *Holmsflat*, a little below that village, and concluded our tour at *Beverey*, the hoſpitable ſeat of doctor *Naſh*, about three miles diſtant.

1784.

In 1784 appeared my letter from a *Welſh* freeholder to his repreſentative, to convert him from his political tenets. My then opinion of the miniſter is daily vindicated.

A WORK deſigned to comprehend the ZOOLOGY of *North America* had long employed my mind and my pen, on which I intended to have beſtowed that name; but, for the affecting rea-

ſon

fon given in the advertifement prefixed to that work, (altered, indeed, from its original plan) I thought myfelf under the neceffity of changing the title. I did fo; and, after having confiderably enlarged the work by the addition of the animals and hiftory of the northern parts of *Europe* and *Afia*, I this year gave it to the public, under the title of the *Arctic Zoology*. It confifts of two volumes, quarto; the firft contains a long introduction, and Clafs I. QUADRUPEDS; the fecond, Clafs II. BIRDS. In this work I received confiderable improvements from the voyage of Sir *Jofeph Banks*, to *Newfoundland*, in 1767. He added greatly to the ornithology by the communication of feveral new fpecies of birds, and feveral other fubjects.

1785.
ARCTIC ZOO-
LOGY.

THIS work was fpeedily tranflated into *German* by profeffor *Zimmerman*, and publifhed in two volumes, quarto, with the prints, which I permitted to be taken from my plates. The introduction was alfo tranflated into *French*, under the title of *Le Nord du Globe*, in two volumes, octavo; and, what is peculiarly flattering to me is, that as much as relates to the north of *Europe* is to be tranflated into *Swedifh*, as an introduction to the natural hiftory of that celebrated feat of the votaries of the great *Cybele*.

GERMAN EDI-
TION.

FRENCH.

THE *Arctic Zoology* gave occafion to my being honored, in the year 1791, on *April* 15th, by being elected member of the *American* Philofophical Society at *Philadelphia*, (in the prefidentfhip of *David Rittenhoufe*, efq.) My labors, relative to that vaft continent, were there favorably received: but this honor I efteem as a reward above my merits. There, fcience of every kind begins to flourifh; among others, that of natural hiftory;

in

in which branch I may predict, that my correfpondent and friend doctor *Benjamin Smith Barton* will foon rife into celebrity, and to his pen I truft the many errors, refpecting the zoology of his native country, will be corrected with tendernefs and candor. In regard to the abilities of the fociety, the volumes of its *Philofophical Tranfactions*, already publifhed, are moft inconteftable proofs.

In this year came out a fecond edition of the firft volume of my *Tour in Wales*.

In *May* 1784, I had the diftinguifhed honor of being elected member of the Royal Academy of Sciences at *Stockholm*. In *Sweden* I am favored with the correfpondence of doctor *Thunberg* of *Upfal*, doctor *Sparman* of *Stockholm*, Mr. *Wilcke* of the fame city, and Mr. *Odman* of *Wormden*, not remote from *Stockholm*. I muft not forget a grateful tribute to the memory of departed friends, to that of baron de *Geer*, profeffor *Wallerius*, and above all doctor *Solander*; the laft fo diftinguifhed by urbanity of manners, and liberality of communication of the infinite knowlege he poffeffed.

On *Jan.* the 3d, 1785, I was elected honorary member of the fociety at *Edinburgh* for promoting of natural knowledge.

On *March* the 5th I received the fame honor from the Society of Antiquaries at *Perth*.

And on *December* the 24th was honored by being elected member of the Agriculture Society, at *Odiham*, in *Hampfhire*.

SUPPLEMENT TO THE ARCTIC ZOOLOGY.

In 1787 I gave a Supplement to the *Arctic Zoology*; it contains feveral additions and corrections, which I owe to the friendfhip of my feveral northern correfpondents, and a fyftematic account

account of the reptiles and fishes of *North America*, together with two very beautiful maps of the countries I had treated of in the introduction, (corrected since the first publication) engraven by that excellent artist Mr. *William Palmer*.

EVER since the year 1777 I had quite lost my spirit of rambling. Another happy nuptial connection suppressed every desire to leave my fire-side. But in the spring of this year I was induced once more to renew my journies. My son had returned from his first tour to the continent, so much to my satisfaction, that I was determined to give him every advantage that might qualify him for a second, which he was on the point of taking over the kingdoms of *France* and *Spain*. I wished him to make a comparison of the naval strength and commercial advantages and disadvantages of our island, with those of her two powerful rivals; I attended him down the *Thames*; visited all our docks; and by land (from *Dartford*) followed the whole coast to the very *Land's End*. On his return from his second tour, I had great reason to boast that this excursion was not thrown away; as to myself it was a painful one; long absence from my family was so new to me, that I may sincerely say it cast an anxiety over the whole journey.

THESE were my greater labors. I, at several times, gave to the public some trifles, which were not ill-received; but few knew the author. These I collected some years ago, and printed, for the amusement of a few friends, thirty copies, by the friendly press of *George Allan*, esq. at *Darlington*.

THE principal was my history of the *Patagonians*, collected from the account given by father *Faulkner*, in 1771, and from the several histories of those people by various writers. I believe

TOUR TO THE
LAND'S END.

MISCELLANIES.

HISTORY OF THE
PATAGONIANS.

5
that

that the authenticity of the feveral relaters is now very well eftablished.   This was printed at the fame prefs, in 1788.

BESIDES thefe may be added, the *ode on indifference*, and the verfes on the lady being chofen patronefs of a hunt and book-club in the fame day.

AN effay on the improper behaviour of married ladies towards our fex, 1774.

A RIDICULE on the bold and mafculine fafhion of the ladies wearing riding-habits at all times of the day; which was republifhed, in 1781, by Mr. *Smith*, with a good mezzotinto of a modern toilet.

AMERICAN annals, an incitement to parlement-men to inquire into the conduct of our commanders in the *American* war.   I omit this paper, unwilling to revive the memory of the moft deplorable event in all the annals of *Great Britain*.

THE *Flintfhire* petition.   The difcontents of the year 1779 were grown to fuch a height, that the county of *Flint* took fhare in the attempt to produce a redrefs of grievances.   I wifhed to allay the popular fury as far as in me lay; becaufe numbers of the complaints were excited by that bane of this kingdom in all ages, pretended patriots.   I formed a fpeech, which I had not courage enough to fpeak, fo printed the lenitive intention, as certainly it could do me no difcredit.   The event fhewed that impoffibilities were attempted, and that foon as the patriots got into power, no more was thought of the plan once urged with much violence.

AN infcription over the entrance of the new gaol at *Flint* is printed in Mr. *Howard*'s account of the principal *Lazarettos* in *Europe*.

THE following grateful epitaph, in memory of my faithful

fervant and friend, *Louis Gold*, may be feen on a fmall brafs plate in *Whiteford* church, clofe to which he was interred, *Auguſt* the 22d, 1785.

> This fmall Monument of efteem
> was erected by his lamenting Mafter
> in Memory of
> LOUIS GOLD,
> a Norman by Birth,
> and above twenty years the faithful
> Servant and Friend
> of THOMAS PENNANT, Efq.
> of Downing.
> In his various fervices
> he made confiderable favings,
> which he difpofed of by his laft will
> (having no relations of his own)
> with affection to his friends
> and to his fellow-fervants,
> with unmerited gratitude to
> his Mafter and his family,
> and
> with piety to the poor.
> Every duty of his humble ſtation,
> and every duty of life,
> he difcharged fo fully,
> That when the day fhall come which levels
> all diftinction of ranks,
> He may,
> By the favour of our bleffed Mediator,
> hear thefe joyful words,

F   " Well

" Well done, thou good and faithful servant,
enter thou into the joy of thy Lord."
He was born at St. Hermes de Rouvelle,
in Normandy, August 22, 1717; died
at Downing, August 20, 1785; and was
interred in the Church-yard near this wall
on the 22d of the same month.

PREVIOUS to this I could not, in the warmth of my heart, resist giving, in one of the *Chester* papers, the following paragraph
as a notification of his death.

'SATURDAY se'nnight, in the morning, died, at *Downing*, in
' *Flintshire, Louis Gold*, a *Norman* by birth, and above twenty years
' the faithful servant and friend of *Thomas Pennant*, of that place,
' esq.   He left the savings of his different services, which were
' very confiderable, to feveral of his friends, his fellow-fervants,
' and to the poor; and bequeathed to his lamenting mafter, and
' his four children, handfome remembrances of his affection for
' them : the remainder to be applied, at the difcretion of his ex-
' ecutor, to charitable ufes.'

1790.
ACCOUNT OF
LONDON.

THIS fpring I publifhed an account of our capital.   I had fo
often walked about the feveral parts of *London*, with my note-
book in my hand, that I could not help forming confiderable
collections of materials.   The public received this work with
the utmoft avidity.   It went through three large impreffions
in about two years and a half.   The firft, in *April* 1790; the
fecond, in *January* 1791; and the third, in the latter end of
the laft year.   Many additions were made to the fecond; together with three more plates by the perfuafion of that worthy

character

character *William Seward*, efq. One was of the buft of *Charles* I. by *Bernini*, which ftood over one of the doors in *Weftminfter-hall*, but was removed on the preparations for the trial of Mr. *Haftings*. I wifh the drawing had been better executed.

In this year Mr. *White* fent into the world a fifth edition of my *Tours in Scotland*, with feveral additions and corrections.

I am often aftonifhed at the multiplicity of my publications, efpecially when I reflect on the various duties it has fallen to my lot to difcharge. As father of a family, landlord of a fmall but very numerous tenantry, and a not inactive magiftrate. I had a great fhare of health during the literary part of my days, much of this was owing to the riding exercife of my extenfive tours, to my manner of living, and to my temperance. I go to reft at ten; and rife winter and fummer at feven, and fhave regular at the fame hour, being a true *mifopogon*. I avoid the meal of excefs, a fupper; and my foul rifes with vigour to its employs, and (I truft) does not difappoint the end of its Creator.

Quin corpus onuftum
Hefternis vitiis, animum quoque prægravat una,
Atque affigit humo divinæ particulam auræ.
Alter, ubi dicto citiùs curata fopori
Membra dedit, vegetus præfcripta ad munia furgit.

Behold how pale the feated guefts arife
From fuppers puzzled with varieties!
The body too, with yefterday's excefs
Burthen'd and tir'd, fhall the pure foul deprefs;
Weigh down this portion of celeftial birth,
This breath of God, and fix it to the earth.

So far refpects my own labors; it will be but juft to men-

F 2   tion

OF OTHERS'
WORKS PRO-
MOTED BY ME.

tion thofe of others, which have been produced by my countenance and patronage; for I never can be accufed of witholding. my communications or my mite to affift my brethren who have wifhed to affume the perilous charaffers of authors.

DOCTOR JOHN
REINHOLD FOR-
STER.

I, VERY early after the arrival of doftor *John Reinhold Forfter*, had opportunity of introducing him to feveral of my friends, which proved of no fmall fervice to him during his refidence in this kingdom. At my perfuafion, and by my encouragement, he tranflated *Kalm's Voyage into North America,* which was publifhed in 1770, in three volumes oftavo.

IN 1771 he publifhed *Ofbeck's Voyage to China,* with that of *Toreen,* and *Eckberg's* account of the *Chinefe* hufbandry, in two volumes.

HE alfo added a fecond volume to his tranflation of *Boffu's Travels in Louifiana,* containing the life of *Loefling,* and a catalogue of *Spanifh* plants, and thofe of part of *Spanifh America.* By thefe the works of three of the moft eminent difciples of the *Linnæan* fchool have been made known to the *Britifh* nation.

I PUBLISHED, at much expence, in 1777, the *Flora Scotica,* in two volumes, oftavo, with xxxvii plates. This was the elaborate work of my worthy friend, and fellow traveller, the rev.

REV. JOHN
LIGHTFOOT.

Mr. *Lightfoot.* The lamented lofs of that admirable botanift, on *February* 20th, 1788, I have related in a fhort account, printed 1788, to be given to the purchafers of the remaining copies of the *Flora Scotica.*

MR. GOUGH.

THAT indefatigable topographer *Richard Gough,* efq. paid me the compliment of fubmitting the fheets of his edition of *Camden,* which related to *North Wales,* to my correftion; and

I flatter

I flatter myfelf that they would not have come out of my hands unimproved. To him I alfo communicated feveral of my manufcript journals, which I flatter myfelf might in fome fmall degree contribute to the improvement of our venerable topographer.

As it was my wifh that no part of *North Britain*, or its iflands, fhould be left unexplored, or any of their advantage loft, for want of notice, I fupported the reverend *Charles Cordiner*, epifcopal minifter at *Banff*, in a journey over the countries north of *Loch Broom*, which I was obliged to defift from attempting; this he performed, much to my fatisfaction, in 1776. I publifhed his journal, entitled, *Antiquities and Scenery of the North of Scotland*, at my own hazard. It is illuftrated with xxii plates, taken from drawings by the fkilful pencil of that ingenious traveller. The work fucceeded. I made him a prefent of the expences which attended his journey.

NUMBERS of other fubjects of antiquities, views, and natural hiftory, are now in publication by the fame gentleman.

I WAS actuated by the fame zeal in refpect to the extreme iflands of the fame parts of our kingdom. In the reverend Mr. *George Low*, minifter of *Birfa* in the *Orknies*, I met with a gentleman willing to undertake the vifitation of thofe iflands, and of the *Schetlands*, and to communicate to me his obfervations of every thing he imagined would be of ufe to the kingdom, or afford me pleafure. His furveys were made in the years 1774 and 1778, and he favored me with a moft inftructive journal, and feveral drawings. It was my wifh to publifh his voyages, as I had the travels of Mr. *Cordiner*; but certain reafons difcouraged me. This ought not to be confidered as

any

REV. CHARLES CORDINER.

REV. GEORGE LOW.

any reflection on the performance. Mr. *Low* gives a good account of the natural hiftory and antiquities of the feveral iflands; enters deeply into their fifheries and commercial concerns; and on the whole is highly worthy the attention of the public.

I CANNOT help mentioning the fervices I did to the profeffors of the art of engraving, by the multitude of plates performed by them for my feveral works; let me enumerate the particulars and total.

Britifh Zoology, folio	—	—	— 132
Britifh Zoology, octavo or quarto	—	— 284
Hiftory of Quadrupeds	—	—	— 54
Tour in Scotland, the three volumes	—	— 134
Journey to London	—	—	— 23
Tour in Wales, two volumes	—	— 53
Mofes Griffith's Supplemental Plates	—	— 10
Some Account of London, fecond edition	—	— 15
Indian Zoology, fecond edition	—	— 17
Genera of Birds	—	—	— 16
Arctic Zoology, two volumes	—	— 26
Syftematic Index to de Buffon	—	—	1
The Rev. Mr. *John Lightfoot's Flora Scotica*, two volumes	37
			802

IF I have omitted Mr. *John Ingleby* of *Halkin, Flintfhire*, I did not do juftice to a very neat drawer. I have often profited of his fervices : and many of the private copies of my works have been highly ornamented by his labors.

NOTWITH-

NOTWITHSTANDING my authorial career was finished on the preceding year, yet no small trouble attends my past labors. The public continues to flatter me with demands for new editions of my works: to the correction and improvement of which, I am obliged to pay confiderable attention. Early this year appeared a new edition of my account of *London*; as I have mentioned at p. 34.

NONE of my acquaintance will deny that I write a moft illegible hand. In order to deliver my labors intelligible to pofterity, on *January* 1ft, of this year, I took into my fervice, as fecretary, *Thomas*, the fon of *Roger Jones*, our parifh-clerk, a worthy, fober, and fteady young man: I determined to profit of his excellent hand-writing to copy my feveral manufcripts, and he has difcharged his duty very much to my fatiffaction.

MR. *White*, at the latter end of this year, printed a third edition of my *Hiftory of Quadrupeds*, with moft of the old plates re-engraven, and feveral new ones. This work was always a favorite one of mine: I beftowed very true pains on it: and added, I may fay, every new animal which has to this time reached the knowlege of the naturalifts.

IN the fpring of the fame year appeared my letter on *Mail Coaches*. I was irrefiftibly compelled to refume my pen, from the oppreffions which the poor labored under, by the demands made on them to repair the roads for the paffage of the mails, with a nicety, and at an expence beyond their powers. Let the little performance fpeak my apology for the publication.

IN

1791.

ACCOUNT OF
LONDON, THIRD
EDITION.

1792.
HISTORY OF
QUADRUPEDS,
THIRD EDITION.

LETTER ON
MAIL COACHES.

INDIAN-ZOOLO-
GY, SECOND EDI-
TION.

IN this year came out a second edition of my *Indian Zoology*, (fee p. 9) but very confiderably enlarged by doctor *Forfter*'s effay prefixed to the *German* edition of that work, which was tranflated by doctor *Aikin*; and by a tolerably complete *Faunula*; a labor taken off my hands principally by the friendfhip of the rev. Mr. *Hugh Davies* and Mr. *Latham*; the *Faunula* of infects fell to Mr. *Latham*, and coft him no fmall pains.

THUS far has paffed my active life, even till the prefent year 1792, in which I have advanced half way of my 67th year. My body may have abated of its wonted vigour; but my mind ftill retains its powers, its longing after improvements, its wifh to receive new lights through chinks which time hath made.

A FEW years ago I grew fond of imaginary tours, and determined on one to climes more fuited to my years, more genial than that to the frozen north. I ftill found, or fancied that I

OUTLINES OF
THE GLOBE.

found, abilities to direct my pen. I determined on a voyage to *India*, formed exactly on the plan of the Introduction to the *Arctic Zoology*; which commences at fuch parts of the north as are acceffible to mortals. From *London* I follow the coafts fouthern to part of our ifland, and from *Calais*, along the oceanic fhores of *Europe*, *Africa*, and *Afia*, till I have attained thofe of *New Guinea*. Refpecting thefe, I have collected every information poffible, from books antient and modern: from the moft authentic, and from living travellers of the moft refpectable characters of my time. I mingle hiftory, natural hiftory, accounts of the coafts, climates, and every thing which I thought could inftruct or amufe. They are written on imperial quarto, and when bound, make a folio of no inconfiderable fize; and are illuftrated, at a vaft expence, by prints taken from books, or

by

by charts and maps, and by drawings by the fkilful hand of *Mofes Griffith*, and by prefents from friends. With the bare poffibility of the volume relative to *India*, none of thefe books are to be printed in my life-time ; but to reft on my fhelves, the amufement of my advancing age. The following is the catalogue of thefe labors, all (excepting the firft) compofed in the fpace of four years, all which will be comprehended under the general title of,

OUTLINES OF THE GLOBE.

Vol. I. will contain the Introduction to the *Arctic Zoology*, with confiderable additions, in order to make it unite hereafter with *China*, which will be comprehended in the xiiith volume ; but this firft volume will alfo be augmented very greatly, by accounts of the internal parts of the country, and with the countries to the fouth, as low as lat. 45, to comprehend the great rivers of the north of *Europe* and *Afia* : not only the coafts but the internal parts of the United States of *America* will be defcribed, as alfo our poor remnant, as far as the mouth of the *Miffiffippi*, and each fide of that vaft river as high as its fource. The plates will be of new fubjects, and executed by the firft engravers of the time : the fize of the books, that of *Cook's Voyages*. I feel an inclination to have one volume publifhed in my life, as a model for the remaining twelve. It was impoffible to omit this *arctic* volume, otherwife the work would have been very imperfect.

Vol. II. defcribes a tour, commencing at the *Temple-ftairs*, comprehending my paffage down the *Thames* as low as *Dartford Creek*, and from thence to *Dover*.

ARCTIC RE-GIONS.

KENTISH TOUR.

G VOL.

FRANCE.

VOL. III. and IV. The voyage along the coasts of *France*, from *Calais* to the frontiers of *Spain*, with a digreffion up the *Loire* as far as *Orleans*; and a fecond digreffion from the *Garonne*, near *Touloufe*, above *Bourdeaux*, along the great canal *de Languedoc*, to its junction with the *Mediterranean* fea near *Sette*; and a third from *Andaye*, along the *French* fide of the *Pyrenees*, as far as its termination on the fame fea.

SPAIN AND POR
TUGAL.

VOL. V. comprehends the coaft of *Spain*, from the *Bidaffao* to the borders of *Portugal*, the whole coaft of *Portugal*; after which thofe of *Spain* are refumed, and continued to the Streights of *Gibraltar*, and its celebrated rock. This volume is particularly rich in drawings (by *Mofes Griffith*) of the birds and fifhes of *Gibraltar*, communicated to me by the rev. the late Mr. *John White*, long refident in that fortrefs.

SOUTHERN
FRANCE.

VOL. VI. contains the entrance into the *Mediterranean* fea, and the fouthern coafts of *Spain*, to the borders of *Italy* at *Nice*, comprehending the coafts of fouthern *France*.

MR. IGNATIUS
D'ASSO.

MR. *Ignatius d'Affo* of *Sarragoffa*, author of the *Zoologia Aragoniæ*, and *Flora* of the fame country, by his intelligent correfpondence, from the year 1783 to the year 1786, furnifhed me with feveral very inftructive materials for the natural hiftory of *Spain*, which were of confiderable fervice in my account of that kingdom. I cannot quit the fubject of the four laft volumes, without (I truft) a moft venial exultation at the fource from whence I drew a confiderable part of my account of the coafts of the kingdoms of *France* and *Spain*; and alfo of fome of the interior country. It would perhaps be affected: but it certainly would be unnatural to fupprefs acknowlegements which fpring warmed from my heart, becaufe I pay them to a fon. *David Pennant*

2

began

began his travels into foreign parts in *Auguſt* 1785; and from that time, (after intervals paſſed at home) has viſited *Switzerland,* the *Griſons* country, all parts of *Italy,* as low as *Pæſtum;* almoſt all *Germany,* and a ſmall part of *Hungary;* *Stiria, Carinthia,* and *Carniola;* almoſt every part of *France,* and much of *Spain.* From his journals, which, now fairly tranſcribed, fill eight folio volumes, I borrowed my moſt authentic materials.

Vol. VII. is an account of the coaſts of northern *Africa,* from *Egypt,* to the ſtreights of *Gibraltar,* and from the ſtreights, along the ſhores of weſtern or atlantic *Africa,* to the *Senegal,* or borders of *Nigritia.* This will include the hiſtory of the great rivers of that vaſt continent, as far as has yet been diſcovered, and in particular that of the *Nile.* Northern Africa,

Vol. VIII. is deſcriptive of the coaſts of *Nigritia,* from the river *Senegal* to *Cape Negro;* and gives an account of the iſle of *Aſcenſion,* and other diſtant iſles. Nigritia.

Vol. IX. takes in the coaſts from *Cape Negro* to the *Cape of Good Hope,* and again the eaſtern coaſts to the entrance of the *Red Sea,* and its ſouthern ſhores as far as the *Iſthmus of Suez;* *Madagaſcar,* and the ſeveral iſles to the eaſt and to the ſouth of that vaſt iſland. Æthiopian Africa.

Vol. X. contains the coaſts of *Arabia* on the *Red Sea,* and on the *Indian* ocean; and on the gulph of *Ormuz* or *Perſian* gulph. Some account of the river *Euphrates,* and the moſt remarkable places from its ſource to its mouth. The coaſts of *Perſia,* within the gulph, and on the *Indian* ocean, to the limits of *Perſia,* as divided from that empire by the river *Indus.* In this volume will be introduced accounts of ſeveral places mentioned in holy writ. Arabia. Persia.

Vol. XI. gives an account of the river *Indus* from its ſource; India.

of

of the *Penjab*; of the weſtern or *Malabar* coaſt of *India* to *Cape Comorin*; of the kingdom of *Madura*, and of the iſland of *Ceylon*.

VOL. XII. deſcribes the eaſtern coaſt of *India*, quite to the mouths of the *Ganges*; and contains an account of that river from its ſources, and the ſeveral great rivers which fall into it; and of the *Burrampooter*, which, after an equal courſe, and vaſt deviation, falls into the *Ganges* juſt before it reaches the ſea. In theſe volumes, much hiſtory (party and controverſy avoided) will be given in their proper places.

VOL. XIII. reſumes the ſubject at *Arracan*, the firſt kingdom in the *India* beyond *Ganges*. Thoſe of *Ava*, *Pegu*, *Lower Siam*, the archipelago of *Mergui*, the *Andaman* and *Nicobar* iſles, are deſcribed. Then follow the ſtreights of *Malacca*, and its peninſula on both ſides; the gulph of *Siam*, and the *Upper Siam*; the celebrated *Ponteamas*, *Cambodia*, *Pulo Condor*, *Ciampa*, *Cochin-China*, and the bay and kingdom of *Tonquin*. The two laſt favor ſo much of *China*, that it is in compliment to the common geographical diviſion that I do not place them out of the limits of *India*. The vaſt and amazing empire of *China*, comes next: future times will read it fully explored by the nobleman ſo judiciouſly ſelected for performing the celebrated embaſſy now on its way. The ſeveral countries dependent on *China*, bordering on the northern and north-weſtern ſides, the iſlands of *Japan*, and the land of *Jeſo*, conclude this volume.

VOL. XIV. The vaſt inſular regions of *India* form the xivth volume, comprehending the great *Malaye* iſlands, ſuch as *Sumatra*, *Java*, *Balli*, *Banca*, *Madura*, and others of leſs note. *Cumbava*, *Flores*, *Timor*, or the iſles which ſtretch eaſt of *Balli*, to

the

the ifles of *Arrou*, not very remote from the coaft of *New Guinea.*

AFTERWARDS are mentioned *Borneo*, and *Celebes* or *Macaffar*; and to the north of them, the *Manilla* or *Philippine* ifles; and to the eaft the rich archipelago of the fpicy ifles, comprehending the *Banda* and the *Moluccas*, and others which may fairly be ranged under that general name. *New Holland*, and *New Guinea*, with its appendages, *New Britain* and *New Ireland*, conclude this important lift. *New South Wales*, or the weftern portion of *New Holland*, is as fully defcribed as poffible: the tranfient wonder of the vaft views of the *Britifh* nation, which, annihilating time and fpace, has dared a plan, which would make other countries ftartle at the very idea.

BORNEO.

THE SPICY ISLANDS.

NEW HOLLAND. NEW GUINEA.

A FAR more complete *Flora* of *India* (than any that has yet appeared) will follow thefe three volumes, as a feparate work, with fmall hiftorical notations, and references to the beft authors on the fubject. It certainly will prove the beft *Linnæan* index to *Rumphius*, and others of the greater *Indian* botanifts.

THE reader may fmile at the greatnefs of the plan, and my boldnefs in attempting it at fo late a period of life. I am vain enough to think that the fuccefs is my vindication. Happy is the age that could thus beguile its fleeting hours, without injury to any one, and, with the addition of years, continue to rife in its purfuits. But more interefting, and ftill more exalted fubjects, muft employ my future fpan.

APPENDIX,

APPENDIX, Nº 1.

TO

THE HONORABLE

DAINES BARRINGTON.

DEAR SIR,

I NOW execute the promife I made in town fome time ago, of communicating to you the refult of my vifit to Mr. *Falkener*, an antient jefuit, who had paffed thirty eight years of his life in the fouthern part of *South America*, between the river *la Plata* and the ftreights of *Magellan*. Let me endeavor to prejudice you in favor of my new friend, by affuring you, that by his long intercourfe with the inhabitants of *Patagonia*, he feems to have loft all *European* guile, and to have acquired all the fimplicity, and honeft impetuofity, of the people he has been fo long converfant with. I venture to give you only as much of his narrative as he could vouch for the authenticity of; which confifts of fuch facts as he was eye-witnefs to, and fuch as will (I believe) eftablifh paft contradiction the veracity of our late circum

navigators,

navigators, and give new lights into the manners of this fingular
race of men: it will not, I flatter myfelf, be deemed imperti-
nent to lay before you a chronological mention of the feveral
evidences that will tend to prove the exiftence of a people of a
fupernatural height inhabiting the fouthern tract. You will
find that the majority of voyagers, who have touched on that
coaft, have feen them, and made reports of their fize, that will
very well keep in countenance the verbal account given by Mr.
Byron, and the printed by Mr. *Clarke:* you will obferve, that if
the old voyagers did exaggerate, it was through the novelty and
amazement at fo fingular a fight; but the latter, forewarned by
the preceding accounts, feem to have made their remarks with
coolnefs, and confirmed them by the experiment of meafure-
ment.

A. D. 1519. The firft who faw thefe people was the great
Magellan; one of them juft made his appearance on the banks of
the river *la Plata,* and then made his retreat: but during *Magellan's* long ftay at *Port St. Julian,* he was vifited by numbers of
this tall race. The firft approached him, finging, and flinging
the duft over his head; and fhewed all figns of a mild and
peaceable difpofition: his vifage was painted; his garment the
fkin of fome animal neatly fewed; his arms a ftout and thick
bow, a quiver of long arrows feathered at one end, and armed
at the other with flint. The height of thefe people was about
feven feet, *(French)* but they were not fo tall as the perfon who
approached them firft, who is reprefented to have been of fo
gigantic a fize, that *Magellan's* men did not with their heads
reach as high as the waift of this *Patagonian.* They had with
them beafts of burden, on which they placed their wives; by

Magellan's

Magellan's defcription of them, they appear to have been the animals now known by the name of *Llama*.

THESE interviews ended with the captivating two of the people, who were carried away in two different fhips; but as foon as they arrived in the hot climate each of them died.

I DWELL the longer on this account, as it appears extremely deferving of credit; as the courage of *Magellan* made him incapable of giving an exaggerated account through the influence of fear: nor could there be any miftake about the height, as he had not only a long intercourfe with them, but the actual poffeffion of two, for a very confiderable fpace of time *.

IT was *Magellan* who firft gave them the name of *Patagons*, becaufe they wore a fort of flipper made of the fkin of animals: *Tellement*, fays *M. de Broffe* †, quils, *paroiffoit avoir des pattes de Bêtes.*

IN 1525, *Garcia de Louifa* faw, within the ftreights of *Magellan*, favages of a very great ftature, but he does not particularife their height.

AFTER *Louifa* the fame ftreights were paffed in 1535 by *Simon de Alcazova*, and attempted in 1540, by *Alphonfo de Camargo*, but without being vifited by our tall people.

THE fame happened to our countryman fir *Francis Drake*; but, becaufe it was not the fortune of that able and popular feaman

* Vide *Ramufios* Coll. Voyages, *Venice* 1550; alfo the letter of *Maximilian Tranfylvanus*, Sec. to *Charles* V. and in the 1ft vol. p. 376. A. and B.

† This account (as well as the others where I do not quote my authority) are taken from that judicious writer *M. de Broffe*.

to meet with thefe gigantic people, his contemporaries confidered the report as the invention of the *Spaniards*.

In 1579, *Pedro Sarmiento* afferts, that thofe he faw were
three ells high. This is a writer I would never venture to quote
fingly, for he deftroys his own credibility by faying, the favage
he made prifoner was an errant *Cyclops:* I only cite him to prove
that he had fell in with a tall race, though he mixes fable with
truth.

In 1586, our countryman, fir *Thomas Cavendifh*, in his voyage,
had only opportunity of meafuring one of their footfteps, which
was eighteen inches long: he alfo found their graves, and mentions their cuftoms of burying near the fhore *.

In 1591, *Anthony Knevet*, who failed with fir *Thomas Cavendifh* in his fecond voyage, relates, that he faw, at *Port Defire*,
men fifteen or fixteen fpans high, and that he meafured the bodies of two that had been recently buried, which were fourteen
fpans long †.

1599.—*Sebald de Veert*, who failed with admiral *de Cordes*, was
attacked in the ftreight *Magellan* by favages whom he thought
to be ten or eleven feet high: he adds, that they were of reddifh
color, and had long hair ‡.

In the fame year *Oliver du Nort*, a *Dutch* admiral, had a ren-
contre with this gigantic race, whom he reprefents to be of a
high ftature and of a terrible afpect.

---

* *Purchas*, i. 58.
† *Purchas*, i. 1232.
‡ Col. Voy. by the *Dutch Eaft India* company, &c. *London* 1703. p. 319.

1614.

1614.—*George Spilbergen*, another *Dutchman*, in his paſſage through the ſame ſtreight, ſaw a man, of a gigantic ſtature, climbing a hill as if to take a view of the ſhip *.

1615.—*Le Maire* and *Schouten* diſcovered ſome of the burying places of the *Patagonians* beneath heaps of great ſtones, and found in them ſkeletons ten or eleven feet long †.

Mr. *Falkener* ſuppoſes, that formerly there exiſted a race of *Patagonians* ſuperior to theſe in ſize; for ſkeletons are often found of far greater dimenſions, particularly about the river *Texeira.* Perhaps he may have heard of the old tradition of the natives mentioned by *Cieza* ‡, and repeated from him by *Garcilaſſo de la Vega* §, of certain giants having come by ſea, and landed near the *Cape of St. Helena*, many ages before the arrival of the *Europeans.*

1618.—*Gracias de Nodal*, a *Spaniſh* commander, in the courſe of his voyage, was informed by *John Moore*, one of his crew, who landed between *Cape St. Eſprit*, and *Cape St. Arenas*, on the ſouth ſide of the ſtreights, that he trafficked with a race of men taller, by the head, than the *Europeans.* This, and the next, are the only inſtances I ever met with of the tall race being found on that ſide of the ſtreights.

1642.—*Henry Brewer*, a *Dutch* admiral, obſerved in the ſtreights *le Maire*, the footſteps of men which meaſured eighteen inches, this is the laſt evidence in the 17th century of the ex-

* *Purchas*, i. 80.
† Ibid. i. 91.
‡ Seventeen years travels of *Peter de Cieza*, 138.
§ Tranſlated by *Ricaut*, p. 263.

iſtence

iftence of thefe tall people: but let it be obferved, that out of the fifteen firft voyagers who paffed through the *Magellanic* ftreights, not fewer than nine are undeniable witneffes of the fact we would eftablifh.

IN the prefent century I can produce but two evidences of the exiftence of the tall *Patagonians*. The one in 1704, when the crew of a fhip belonging to *St. Maloe's*, commanded by captain *Harrington*, faw feven of thefe giants in *Gregory* bay. Mention is alfo made of fix more being feen by captain *Carman*, a native of the fame town; but whether in the fame voyage my authority is filent *.

BUT as it was not the fortune of the four other voyagers †, who failed through the ftreights in the 17th century, to fall in with any of this tall race, it became a fafhion to treat as fabulous the account of the preceding nine, and to hold this lofty race as the mere creation of a warm imagination.

IN fuch a temper was the public, on the return of Mr. *Byron* from his circumnavigation, in the year 1766. I had not the honor of having perfonal conference with that gentleman, therefore will not repeat the accounts I have been informed he had given to feveral of his friends; I rather chufe to recapitulate that given by Mr. *Clarke* ‡, in the *Philofophical Tranfactions* for 1767, p. 75. Mr. *Clarke* was officer in Mr. *Byron's* fhip, landed with him in the ftreights of *Magellan*, and had for two

---

* *Frezier's Voy.* 84.

† Sir *John Narborough*, in 1670; *Bartholomew Sharp*, in 1680; *De Gennes*, in 1696; and *Beauchefne Gouin*, in 1699.

‡ This able officer commanded the *Difcovery* in captain *Cook's* laft voyage, and died off *Kamtfchatka*, *Auguft* 22, 1779.

hours

hours an opportunity of ſtanding within a few yards of this race, and ſeeing them examined and meaſured by Mr. *Byron*. He repreſents them in-general as ſtout and well proportioned, and aſſures us, that none of the men were lower than eight feet, and that ſome even exceeded nine; and that the women were from ſeven feet and an half to eight feet. He ſaw Mr. *Byron* meaſure one of the men, and, notwithſtanding the commodore was near ſix feet high, he could, when on tip-toe, but juſt reach with his hand the top of the *Patagonian*'s head; and Mr. *Clarke* is certain, that there were ſeveral taller than him on whom the experiment was made, for there were about five hundred men, women, and children. They ſeemed very happy at the landing of our people, and expreſſed their joy by a rude ſort of ſinging. They were of a copper color, and had long lank hair, and faces hideouſly painted; both ſexes were covered with ſkins, and ſome appeared on horſeback and others on foot.

M. de Premontel makes this an object of ridicule, as if the ſize of the horſes were unequal to the burden of the riders. Our navigators tell us, that the horſes were fifteen or ſixteen hands high. It is well known, that a mill-horſe has been known to carry nine hundred and ten pounds, a weight probably beyond that of any *Patagonian* they ſaw.

A FEW had on their legs a ſort of boot, with a ſharp-pointed ſtick at the heel inſtead of a ſpur. Their bridles were made of thong, the bit wood; the ſaddle as artleſs as poſſible, and without ſtirrups. The introduction of horſes into theſe parts by the *Europeans*, introduced likewiſe the only ſpecies of manufacture they appear to be acquainted with. All their ſkill ſeems to extend no farther than theſe rude eſſays at a harneſs;

and

and to equip themſelves for *Cavaliers*. In other reſpects they would be in the ſame ſtate as our firſt parents juſt turned out of paradiſe, cloathed in coats of ſkins; or at beſt in the ſame condition in which *Cæſar* found the ancient *Britons*; for their dreſs was ſimilar, their hair long, and their bodies, like thoſe of our anceſtors, made terrific by wild painting. Theſe people, by ſome means or other, had acquired a few beads and bracelets; otherwiſe not a ſingle article of *European* fabric appeared among them. Theſe they muſt have gotten by the intercourſe with the other *Indian* tribes: for had they had any intercourſe with the *Spaniards*, they never would have neglected procuring knives, the ſtirrups, and other conveniences which the people ſeen by Mr. *Wallis* had.

I ſHOULD have been glad to have cloſed, in this place, the relations of this ſtupendous race of mankind; becauſe the two following accounts given by gentlemen of character and abilities ſeem to contradict great part of what had been before advanced, or at leſt ſerve to give ſcoffers room to ſay, that the preceding navigators had ſeen theſe people through the medium of magnifying glaſſes, inſtead of the ſober eye of obſervation: but before I make my remarks on what has been before related, I ſhall proceed with the other navigators, and then attempt to reconcile the different accounts. In 1767, captain *Wallis* of the *Dolphin*, and captain *Philip Carteret* of the *Swallow* ſloop, ſaw and meaſured with a pole ſeveral of the *Patagonians*, who happened to be in the ſtreights of *Magellan* during his paſſage *, he repreſents them as a fine and friendly people, cloathed in ſkins,

---

* *Phil. Tranſ.* 1770, p. 21. *Hawkeſworth's Voy.* i. 374.

and

and on their legs a fort of boots, and many of them tied their hair, which was long and black, with a fort of woven ftuff of the breadth of a garter, made of fome kind of wool. That their arms were flings formed of two round balls, faftened one to each end of a cord, which they fling with great force and dexterity. He adds, they hold one ball in their hand, and fwing the other at the full length of the cord round their head, by which it acquires a prodigious velocity: they will fling it to a great diftance, and with fuch exactnefs, as to ftrike a very fmall object. Thefe people were alfo mounted on horfes; their faddles, bridles, &c. were of their own making; fome had iron, and others metal bits to their bridles, and one had a *Spanifh* broad fword; but whether the laft articles were taken by war, or procurred by commerce, is uncertain; but the laft is moft probable. It feems evident that they had intercourfe with *Europeans*, and had even adopted fome of their fafhions; for many had cut their drefs into form of *Spanifh Punchos*, or a fquare piece of cloth with a hole cut for the head, the reft hanging loofe as low as the knees. They alfo wore drawers; fo thefe people had attained a few fteps farther towards civilifation than their gigantic neighbors; others again will appear to have made a far greater advance; for thefe ftill devoured their meat raw, and drank nothing but water.

M. *Bougainville*, in the fame year, faw another party of the natives of *Patagonia:* he meafured feveral of them, and declares that none were lower than five feet five inches, *French*, or taller than five feet ten; *i. e.* five feet ten, or fix feet three, *Englifh* meafure. He concludes his account with faying, that he afterwards

wards met with a taller people in the South Sea, but I do not recollect that he mentions the place.

I AM sorry to be obliged to remark, in these voyages, a very
illiberal propensity to cavil at and invalidate the account given by
Mr. *Byron*: but at the same time exult in having had an opportunity given me by that gentleman of vindicating his and the national
honor. *M. Bougainville*, in order to prove he fell in with the
identical people that Mr. *Byron* conversed with, asserts, that he
saw numbers of them possessed of knives of an *English* manu-
factory, certainly given them by Mr. *Byron*; but he should have
considered that there are more ways than one of coming at a
thing, that the commerce between *Sheffield* and *South America*,
through the port of *Cadiz*, is most uncommonly large; and that
his *Indians* might have got their knives from the *Spaniards* at the
same time that they got their gilt nails and *Spanish* harness: but
for farther satisfaction on this subject, I have liberty to say, from
Mr. *Byron*'s authority, that he never gave a single knife to the
people he saw; that he had not one at that time about him;
that, excepting the presents given with his own hands, and the
tobacco brought by lieutenant *Cummins*, not the left trifle was
bestowed. I am furnished with one other proof, that these lesser
Indians, whom Mr. *Wallis* saw, were not the same with those
described by Mr. *Byron*, as has been insinuated: for the first
had with him some officers who had been with him on the preceding voyage, and who bear witness, not only to the difference
of size, but declare that these people had not a single article
among them given by Mr. *Byron**. It is extremely probable

* See Mr. *Byron*'s letter at the end.

that

that thefe were the *Indians* that Mr. *Bougainville* fell in with; for they were furnifhed with bits, a *Spanifh* fcymeter, and brafs ftir-rups as before mentioned.

My laft evidence of thefe gigantic *Americans* is that which I received from Mr. *Falkener*; he acquainted me, that about the year 1742 he was fent on a miffion to the vaft plains of *Pampas*, which, if I recollect right, lie to the fouth-weft of *Buenos Ayres*, and extend near a thoufand miles towards the *Andes*. In thefe plains he firft met with fome tribes of thefe people, and was taken under the protection of one of the *Caziques*. The remarks he made on their fize were as follows; that the talleft, which he meafured in the fame manner that Mr. *Byron* did, was feven feet eight inches high; that the common height, or middle fize, was fix feet; that there were numbers that were even fhorter; and that the talleft women did not exceed fix feet. That they were fcattered from the foot of the *Andes,* over that vaft tract which extends to the *Atlantic Ocean,* and are found as far as the *Red River* at *Bay Anagada,* lat. 40. 1; below that the land is too barren to be habitable, and none are found, except accidental migrants, till you arrive at the river *Gallego,* near the ftreights of *Magellan.*

They are fuppofed to be a race derived from the *Chilian In-dians,* the *Puelches* who inhabited the eaftern fide of the *Andes,* the fame brave nation who defeated and deftroyed the avari-cious *Spaniard Baldivia,* but after that were difpoffeffed of their feat.

They dwell in large tents covered with the hides of mares, and divided within into apartments, for the different ranks of the family, by a fort of blanketing. They are a moft migratory

I   people,

people, and often fhift their quarters; when the women ftrike the tents, affift in putting them on their horfes, and, like the females of all favage countries, undergo all the laborious work.

They have two motives for fhifting their quarters; one, for the fake of getting falt, which they find incrufted in the fhallow pools near the fea fide.

The other inducement is the fuperftition they have of burying their dead within a certain diftance of the ocean. And I may certainly add a third, that of the neceffity they muft lie under of feeking frefh quarters on account of the chace, which is their principal fubfiftence.

Those who deny the exiftence of thefe great people, never confider the migratory nature of the inhabitants of this prodigious tráct, and never reflect that the tribes who may have been feen this month on the coaft, may the next be fome hundreds of miles inland, and their place occupied by a tribe or nation totally different. Thefe gentlemen feem to lay down as a certain pofition, that *Patagonia* is peopled by only a fingle nation; and from that falfe principle they draw their arguments, fneer, infult, and even grofsly abufe all that differ in opinion. Among the moft illiberal of thefe writers is *M. de Premontal*, who, with the rapid ingenuity of his country, mounts on his headftrong courfer Prejudice, fets off full fpeed, rides over all the honeft fellows that would inform him of his road, and fpurns even Truth herfelf, though fhe offers to be his guide: but truth is unadorned, and hated by this fantaftic writer; it would fpoil him of all the flowers of fiction, and tropes of abufe, againft a rival country; and would teach him facts that would ruin his argument,

2.   and

and reduce his eloquent *memoire* to a fingle narrative of un-contefted veracity.

THEIR food is (almoft entirely) animal : the flefh of horfes, oxen, guanacoes, and oftriches, all of which they eat roafted or boiled. Their drink is water, except in the feafon when certain fpecies of fruit are ripe, for of thofe they make a fort of fermenting liquor called *Chucha*, common to many parts of *South America*. One kind is made of a podded fruit called *Algarrova*, which fmells like a bug, and when bruifed in water becomes an inebriating liquor. The fame fruit is alfo eaten as bread. The other *Chucha* is made of the *Molie*, a fmall fruit, hot and fweet in the mouth : both thefe caufe a deep drunken-nefs, efpecially the laft, which excites a phrenetic inebriation, and a wildnefs of eyes, which lafts two or three days.

THE cloathing of thefe people is either a mantle of fkins, or of a woollen * cloth manufactured by themfelves; fome is fo ftrong and compact as even to hold water: the color is various, for fome are ftriped and dyed with the richeft red, made of cochineal and certain roots. They wear a fhort apron before, which is tucked between the legs, and preferves a modeft appearance. They never wear feathered ornaments, except in their dances. Their hair is long, and tied up with a fillet. They have naturally beards †, but they generally pluck up the hairs; not but fome leave muftaches, as was obferved by Mr. *Carteret* and *M. Bougainville*.

* The *Puelches* have no fheep but what they purchafe from the *Voluches*, who inhabit the *Andes*, cultivate fheep, and raife corn; the wool is equally fine with that of *Old Spain*.

† *M. Premontal* roundly afferts that they have no beards.

I 2 WHEN

WHEN they go to war, they wear a fourfold coat, of the skin of the *Tapiir*, a cap of bull's hide doubled, and a broad target of the same. Their offensive weapons are bows and arrows, the last headed with bone, lances headed with iron, and broad swords, both which they procure from the *Spaniards*: but their native weapons are slings; of these they have two kinds; one for war, which consists of a thong, headed with stone at only one end; and during their campaigns they carry numbers of these wrapped about their bodies.

THE slings which they use in the chace of horses, cattle, or ostriches, have a stone fixed to each end; and sometimes another thong, with a third stone, is fastened to the middle of the other: these, with amazing dexterity, they fling round the objects of the chace, be they beasts or ostriches, which entangle them so that they cannot stir. The *Indians* leave them, I may say thus tied neck and heels, and go on in pursuit of fresh game; and, having finished their sport, return to the animals they left secured in the slings.

THEIR wars are chiefly with the other *Indians*, for *Patagonia* is inhabited by variety of people, not a single nation. They have a great deal of intercourse with the *Spaniards*, and often come down to *Buenos Ayres* to trade for iron, bugles, &c.

THIS commerce with the *Europeans* has corrupted them greatly, taught them the vice of dram-drinking, and been a dreadful obstacle to their moral improvement. Mr. *Falkener* informed me, that he once prevaled on about five hundred to form a reduction, but that they grew unruly and ungovernable as soon as the *Spanish* traders got among them.

THEIR war and their chace are carried on on horseback, for

they

they are moſt expert riders, and have multitudes of horſes, with which the country is perfectly over-run, for they go in herds of thouſands. The price of a horſe at preſent is two dollars, or 9 s. and 2 d. provided it has been broken.. About the year 1554[*], near the time of the conqueſt of *Peru*, the common price of one was from four to ſix thouſand to ten thouſand *Peſos* [†], or from £.1350 to £.2250 *Engliſh*.

THE venereal diſtemper is common among them. They do not ſpeak. of it as an exotic diſorder; ſo probably it is aboriginal.

IN reſpect to religion, they allow two principles, a good and a bad [‡]. The good they call, the Creator of all things; but conſider him as one that, after that, never ſolicits himſelf about them. He is ſtyled by ſome *Soucha*, or chief in the land of ſtrong drink; by others *Gauyara-cunnee*, or Lord of the dead. The evil principle is called *Hueccovoe*, or the wanderer without. Sometimes theſe (for there are ſeveral) are ſuppoſed to preſide over particular perſons, protect their own people, or injure others. Theſe are likewiſe called *Valichu*, or dwellers in the air.

THEY have prieſts and prieſteſſes, whoſe office is to mediate with theſe beings in caſe of ſickneſs or any diſtreſs; by the intervention of the prieſt they are conſulted about future events; at thoſe ſeaſons the prieſt ſhuts himſelf up, and falls into a phre--

---

[*] *Garcilaſſa de la Vega*, 377, *Engl.* tranſlation.

[†] *Peſos* in the original; perhaps *Peſos duros*, which makes the above ſum..

[‡] *M. de Premontal* is clear they have no ſort of religion.

netic extacy *, and appears epileptic.   If he gives a wrong an-
fwer, he lays the fault on the evil principle, who, he fays, had deceived him by not coming in perfon, but only fent one of his
flaves.   At thefe times the great people affemble about the
cabin, from whence the oracle is to be delivered, waiting its report with great anxiety.

IF a *Cazique* dies, or any public calamity happens; for example, in particular, when the fmall-pox had made great ravages
among the tribes, the priefts are fure to fuffer, for the misfor-
tune is prefumed to have happened through their neglect in not
deprecating the evil; in thefe cafes they have no other method
of faving themfelves, but by laying the blame on others of their
brethren.

PRIESTS are chofen from among the young people, the moft
effeminate they can find; but thofe that are epileptic have always the preference, and thefe drefs in a female habit.

THE *Puelches* have a notion of a future ftate, and imagine that
after death they are to be tranfported to a country, where the
fruits of inebriation are eternal, there to live in immortal drunk-
ennefs, or the perpetual chace of the oftrich.

WHEN a perfon of eminence dies, the moft refpectable woman in the place goes into the tent, clears the body of all the
inteftines, and fcrapes off as much of the flefh from the bones
as poffible, and then burns very carefully both that and the en-
trails: when that is done, the bones are buried till the reft of
the flefh is quite decayed; they are taken up within a year;

---

* The pretenders to fecond fight, in the *Hebrides*, and the *Awenyddion*, or the
Infpired, among the *Welch*, are feized with the fame extafies.

and

and if any of the bones drop out of their places they are refixed and tied together, and the whole formed into a perfect ſkeleton. Thus complete, it is packed up in a hide, put on the back of a favorite horſe of the deceaſed, and then tranſlated to the tomb of his anceſtor, perhaps 300 miles diſtant, and always within a ſmall ſpace from the ſea.

THE ſkeleton is then taken out, and, decked in its beſt robes, and adorned with plumes and beads, is placed ſitting in a deep ſquare pit, parallel with thoſe buried before, with ſword, lance, and other weapons placed by them; and the ſkins of their horſes, ſtuffed, and ſupported by ſtakes, alſo accompany them. The top of the pit is then covered with turf, placed on tranſverſe beams.

A MATRON is appointed to attend theſe ſepulchres, whoſe office it is to keep the ſkeletons clean, and to new-clothe them annually*. I forgot to add, that, on depoſiting a ſkeleton in its tomb, the *Puelches* make a libation of *Chucha*, and, like what I have heard of an honeſt *Spaniard*, drink *Viva el morte*, Long live the dead.

THEY allow polygamy, and marry promiſcuouſly among other *Americans*; they are allowed as many as three wives apiece, but if any take more than that number, he is eſteemed a libertine, and held in very little eſteem.

WIDOWS black their faces for a year after their huſbands deceaſe.

IN reſpect to government, the *Caziques* are hereditary, it is

---

* This account agrees with thoſe given by *Lafitau* in moſt particulars; vide *Mœurs des Sauvages*, xi. 438.

their

their bufinefs to protect the property of their people, and they
have power of life and death : the office is far from being eli-
gible ; many reject it, becaufe they are obliged to pay all their
people for their fervices, who may at pleafure change their
Caziques, fo that feveral refufe to accept new vaffals, who may
offer themfelves ; for it is not allowed any *Indian* to live out of
the protection of fome *Cazique:* in fuch a cafe he would certainly be looked on as an outlaw.

ELOQUENCE is in high efteem with them.   If a *Cazique* wants
that talent, he keeps an orator; juft as leaders in oppofition
have been known to do among us.

THIS clofes the hiftory Mr. *Falkener* favored me with; but
I muft not quit that gentleman without informing you, that he
returned to *Europe* with a fuit of *Patagonian* cloth, a cup of
horn, and a little pot made of *Chilian* copper ; the whole fruits
the *Spaniards* left him, after the labors of a thirty-eight years
miffion.

FROM the preceding account it appears, that the country,
which goes under the name of *Patagonia*, extending from the
river *la Plata*, lat. 35, to the ftreights of *Magellan*, lat. 53 *,
and weftward as far as the *Andes*, is inhabited by men who may
be divided into three different claffes ; and to them may be added
a fourth, a combination or mixture of others.

THE firft is a race of men of common fize, who have been
feen by numbers, and whofe exiftence is indifputable.   Thefe
often are feen on the northern fide of the ftreights of *Magellan*,

---

* M. *de Premontal* will compare *Patagonia* to the fpace between the *Riviere
des Sardines* and the ftreights of *Magellan.*

and

and oftener on the *Terra del Fuego* fide, even as low as oppofite to *Cape Horn*. Thefe are frequently an exiled race, unhappy fugitives, drove by their enemies to take fhelter from their fury, in thofe diftant parts; for fuch is the information Mr. *Falkener* received from fome *Indians* he met with in the fouthern parts of *Patagonia*, and this will account for the fettled melancholy of the people obferved by the navigators in *Terra del Fuego*.

THE fecond clafs confifts of thofe who (in general) exceed the common height of *Europeans* by a few inches, or perhaps the head; fuch were thofe who were feen by *John Moore*, who failed with *Gracias de Nodal*, in 1618; by Mr. *Carteret*, in 1767, and by *M. Bougainville*, in the fame year.

THE third clafs is compofed of thofe whofe height is fo extraordinary as to occafion fo great a difbelief of the accounts of voyagers; and yet they are indifputably an exiftent people; they have been feen by *Magellan*, and fix others, in the 16th century, and by two if not three in the prefent.

THE fourth clafs is a mixed race, who, carelefs about preferving their generous and exalted breed pure and undegenerate, have degraded themfelves by intermixing with the puny tribes of the country, and from that intercourfe have produced a mongrel breed of every fize, except that of the original ftandard; fome few, as if by accident, feem to afpire to the height of their anceftors, but are checked in their growth, and ftop at the ftature of feven feet eight inches, fcarce the middle fize of the genuine breed. But another reafon may be affigned for the degeneracy and inequality of fize in this clafs: they live within the neighborhood of *Europeans*, they have intercourfe with them, and from them they have acquired the vice of dram-drinking,

K   and

and all its horrible confequences; this alone is fufficient to make a nation of giants dwindle into pygmies.

A THIRD reafon may ftill be affigned, viz. the introduction of manufactories among them. Thofe people, who depended on the fpoils of the chace for their habiliments, were certain of preferving their full vigor, their ftrength of conftitution, and fulnefs of habit; while thofe who are confined to the loom grow enervate, and lofe much of the force of their bodily faculties. They alfo live in tents lined with woollen manufacture, which doubtlefsly are much more delicate, luxurious, and warm, than the dwellings of the third undegenerate clafs. We are unacquainted with the form of their tents, but we know that they ftill cloath themfelves with the fkins of beafts, and that, among thofe Mr. *Clarke* faw, there was not the leaft appearance of manufactury, excepting what related to their horfe furniture. Thefe feem to have been the genuine remains of the free race; the conquerors of *Pedro de Baldivia*; the *Puelches*, whofe original ftation was among the *Andes* of *Chiloe*, in about latitude 43, and almoft due eaft of the ifle of *Chiloe*. Thefe were the defcendants of the *Indians* who retreated to the fouth, far out of the common track of *Europeans*, and who retain their primeval grandeur of fize: the others, who fled north-eaft, forgetful of their original magnificent ftature, loft in general that noble diftinction by unfuitable alliances, and the ufe of fpirits, while the firft probably only marry among themfelves, and certainly have all ftrong liquor in abhorrence: fome of this tall race feem ftill to inhabit the ftations of their anceftors, or fome not very remote from them; for *M. Frezier* was affured by *Don Pedro Molina*, governor of *Chiloe*, that he once was vifited by

x   fome

fome of thefe people, who were four *varas*, or about nine or ten feet high; they came in company with fome *Chiloe Indians* *, with whom they were friends, and who probably found them in fome of their excurfions.

M. de Premontal infults *M. Frezier* with much acrimony on account of this relation; and charges him with changing the feat of thofe people from the eaftern coaft to the weftern, or the tract between *Chiloe* and the *Magellanic* ftreights; but the truth is, that *Frezier* fays no fuch thing, but mentions them as a nation living up the country inland, not near the fhores; *M. Premontal* alfo fneers at the evidence of the crews of the *Maloe* fhips; but they by no means place thefe tall people on the weftern coaft of *South America*, but at *Gregory Bay*, a place very little diftant from the eaftern entrance of the ftreights, and near which thefe giants have been more frequently feen than any where elfe.

My remarks on *M. de Premontal* are but a tribute to the many civilities I have received from doctor *Matie*, who has been moft unprovokedly, unjuftly, and illiberally abufed by this vague and pragmatical writer.

Thus I conclude all that I collect relating to thefe fingular people. Let me beg you to receive the account with your ufual candor, and think me, with the moft regard,

Dear Sir,

Your faithful and affectionate humble fervant,

THOMAS PENNANT.

Downing, Nov. 28th, 1771.

* *Frezier's Voyage,* page 86.

K 2

Copy

Copy of a paper tranfmitted from admiral *Byron* to me;
through the hands of the right reverend *John Egerton*,
late bifhop of *Durham*, after he had perufed the manufcript of the foregoing account.

" THE people I faw, upon the coaft of *Patagonia*, were not
" the fame that was feen the fecond voyage. One or two of
" the officers that failed with me, and afterwards with captain
" *Wallace*, declared to me that they had not a fingle thing I
" had diftributed amongft thofe I faw. *M. Bougainville* remarks
" that his officers landed amongft the *Indians* I had feen, as
" they had many *Englifh* knives amongft them, which were, as
" he pretends, undoubtedly given by me: now it happened
" that I never gave a fingle knife to any of thofe *Indians*, nor
" did I even carry one afhore with me.

" I HAD often heard from the *Spaniards*, that there were two
" or three different nations of very tall people, the largeft of
" which inhabit thofe immenfe plains at the back of the *Andes*.
" The others fomewhere near the river *Galiegos*. I take it to
" be the former that I faw, and for this reafon :—returning from
" *Port Famine*, where I had been to wood and water, I faw
" thofe peoples' fires a long way to the weftward of where I
" had left them, and a great way inland, fo, as the winter was
" approaching, they were certainly returning to a better cli-
" mate. I remarked that they had not one fingle thing amongft
" them that fhewed they ever had any commerce with *Euro-*
" *peans*. They were certainly of a moft amazing fize: fo much
" were their horfes difproportioned, that all the people that
" were with me in the boats, when very near the fhore, fwore

*

" that

" that they were all mounted upon deer; and to this inftant I
" believe there is not a man that landed with me, though they
" were at fome diftance from them, but would fwear they took
" them to be nine feet high. I do fuppofe many of them were
" between feven and eight, and ftrong in proportion.

" Mr. *Byron* is much obliged to Mr. *Pennant* for the perufal
" of his manufcript, and thinks his remarks very judicious."

APPENDIX,

APPENDIX, N° 2.

FREE THOUGHTS

ON THE

MILITIA LAWS,

ADDRESSED

TO THE POOR INHABITANTS OF

NORTH WALES.

1781.

Stat. L.   *The Statutes at Large, publifhed by*
            Owen Ruffhead, Efq.

Digeft.   *Digeft of the Militia Laws, by*
            Richard Burn, LL.D. 1781.

FREE THOUGHTS, &c.

MY DEAR COUNTRYMEN,

AT a time in which you feel the diftreffes in common with the reft of the nation, it behoves every one of you to be made acquainted with the laws, in order (as much as is poffible) to eafe yourfelves of the burdens under which you labor, and legally to refift every oppreffion which may be attempted againft you.

THE moft grievous load which you now feel (next to the poor's rate) is that which arifes from the taxes to fupport the militia. The laws relating to it are the moft numerous, and the punifhments attending the breach of them are fo hard, that for fear that any of you fhould offend, by reafon of ignorance, I fhall, in the briefeft manner, fet before you a few points which concern perfons in every ftation of life. If I fhould chance to fpeak of any piece of hiftory, or touch on any thing beyond the apprehenfions of any of you, your minifter is, I truft, refident among you, and ready to expound any diffi-culty.

THE militia has been of very long ftanding in this kingdom; feveral ftatutes were from very old times enacted for its regula-tion, which in the reign of *Charles* II. were revifed, and a new body of laws framed. Thefe were continued almoft to the reign of his prefent majefty; for after they had undergone feve-ral alterations in the latter part of his grandfather's time, they

13, 14 Ch. II. c. 3.
Stat. L. iii. 219.
Digeft 1.

30 G. II. c. 25.
Stat. L. viii. 80.

L   were

were totally repealed, and the laws under which we now act were made in their place; but many of the claufes of the preceding ftatute were reftored. The former is called the *Old Militia*. It certainly was of very little ufe as it then ftood;

13, 14 Ch. II.
L. iii. f. 3.

but it had one advantage over the prefent; for the expence of raifing the men was founded on the trueft juftice. Thofe who had great eftates, palaces, and rich furniture to defend, were charged accordingly. The gentlemen of leffer fortune, and free-holders, were charged lefs; and the honeft farmer, who had nothing but his rick-yard, the hard fruit of his labor! his poor dwelling, and his coarfe bed, to care about, was only obliged

The fame, f. 29.
Digeft, p. 8.

to pay according to fuch private agreement as might be made between him and his landlord; and all this was done in the arbitrary reign of a *Stuart!* But at prefent there is, in one inftance, a more levelling principle. The poor laborer is, in

2 G. III. f. 42.
Stat. L. viii. 622.
Digeft 6.

fome cafes, obliged to contribute ten pounds (if he can raife it) towards the defence of the kingdom; and the greateft fquire in the principality is not bound to give a farthing more.

In the *Old Militia*, all bufinefs relating to the charging the fubject with finding foldiers, was committed to the lieutenant of the county and his deputies, or to the major part of thofe

13, 14 Ch. II. c. 3.
f. 3.
Stat. L. iii. 219.
Digeft 3.

prefent; or, in the abfence of the lieutenant, to the major part of the deputy lieutenants then prefent; which major part was to be *three at left*. I am forry to remark, that even at the firft framing of the new militia, this important fecurity of the in-

2 G. III. f. 58.
Stat. L. viii. 624.
18 G. III. c. 59. f. 11.
Stat. L. xiii. 288.
Digeft 47.

terefts of the poor fubject was weakened: for the powers were in that act entrufted to three deputy lieutenants or juftices only; and fince that time, the number (when the militia is in actual fervice) is reduced to two only.

4   THIS

THIS has been a moſt dangerous and imprudent alteration. Every one knows the hazard of truſting power in few hands. Friendſhip, relationſhip, or an unfortunate congenial turn of mind, may be found in two, which will hardly be met with in a greater number. In fact, two may become but as one, and this reduction be productive of the moſt ſhameful abuſes.

BUT if it were poſſible, that a gentleman ſhould ſo far forget the duty he owes to his country, as to adopt a ſyſtem, in the moſt diſtant view productive of a military government; ſhould he, through miſtaken friendſhip, promote or ſecond any illegality of proceeding; Heaven have mercy upon poor *Britain!* Not the increaſing power of the crown; not the machinations of a faction; not the corruption of a parlement, will half ſo effectually ruin its conſtitution. Not the force of man can overturn it, if the civil powers are true to their truſt: nor leſs than the intervention of Heaven preſerve it, if they are falſe.

AT preſent perhaps no danger is to be apprehended; but, for the ſake of poſterity, let us guard againſt events; and remember, that " an attack by ſtorm may be repulſed, but an unſuſpected " ſap is ſure in the end to overturn the ſtrongeſt works."

Is the militia at preſent that pure aſſemblage of men of rank, fortune, and independence, as it was in the beginning? It may conſiſt of perſons of equal integrity. But is it not poſſible that a few may have crept in, deſtitute of qualification, or deſtitute of heads ſteady enough to bear the great trial of power? Are there no inſtances of their carrying the controul of the camp into private life; none, of their ruffling the tranquillity of the ſocial hour, clouding the bright moments of the gay aſſembly; or pre-

L 2   venting

venting the impending nap of the quiet magiftrate, who dared to differ in opinion with them?

I SHALL make no remarks on the method of ballotting, except this: that a power is given to the deputy lieutenants and juf-tices to order a frefh ballot, in cafe the lot falls on any perfon who, by reafon of infirmity, or want of fize, is unfit to ferve. This is extremely juft: yet ftrict attention fhould be paid to this power; leaft through too great nicety in the gentlemen, or too great favor to the commanding officer, they fhould be in-duced to reject thofe to whom nothing but the moft trivial, or perhaps affected objections could be made. Befides, it moft commonly happens, that on the day of appeal the lifts are en-tirely cleared from all objectionable perfons. For the fake of the people therefore, a fevere penalty fhould be enacted, as a guard againft the abufe of this power.

18 G. III. c. 14*.
Digeft, ed. 1778.
p. 52.

IF any of you who are ballotted, do not chufe to ferve, you have liberty of offering a fubftitute; and that fubftitute muft be five feet four inches high, and fit for fervice. You muft offer none but fuch who are active in body and found in mind: who can fully anfwer the purpofe for which they are called out, that of defending our wives, children, and property. You muft offer fuch who will not fhame you in diftant counties, or give needlefs trouble to the gentlemen who command them, and who have, in many inftances, for all our fakes, given up for a time every comfort of a domeftic life.

* Abridged, and part of the claufe omitted, in Mr. *Ruffhead's* edition. See vol. xiii. 181.

IF

IF you happen to be fix feet high, and formed as perfect as man can be, the magiftrates ought not to refufe a fubftitute inferior to you in thofe advantages; it may be your good (or I may fay in this cafe) your ill fortune to be fo made: but ftill they ought not to refufe any one you offer, who comes within the above defcription. Two deputy lieutenants, or one deputy lieutenant and one juftice, have power to accept or refufe them. If thefe two are refolved to plague you, by the refufal of proper fubftitutes, look about the room, and fee if there are any others prefent, and perhaps by their interference the former may be fhamed into compliance; for there are none but have eyes as well as they, to difcern whether a man is five feet four, and proper to be accepted; and fenfe enough to know (in cafes where a fubftitute is accepted) that a fingle man will be lefs burdenfome to a parifh than a married man. A merciful magiftrate will furely never hefitate to prefer the former?

THE poffible abufe of the power of rejection, or acceptance of fubftitutes, when lodged in two only, fhews the neceffity of refuming the antient mode, and of enlarging the number. At prefent, let the power be ever fo much abufed, you are left helplefs in this act, for there is no punifhment for thofe who make fo wanton an exertion of it.

BUT remember, that in cafe you are at length teized, by the refufal of feveral ftout fubftitutes, into the payment of ten pounds (which, properly fpeaking, is only to be levied in cafe you refufe or neglect to provide a man in your room) remember, I fay, that you are to pay the money into the hands of the churchwardens and overfeers of your refpective parifhes only, who are alfo the only perfons appointed by law to receive and pay the

2 G. III. c. 20. f. 42.
Stat. L. viii. 622.
2 G. III. c. 20. f. 51.
Stat. L. viii. 624.
Digeft 57.

ten

ten pounds, or to agree or contract for any fubftitutes, unlefs

2 G. III. c. 20. f. 52.
Digeft 58.

you fhould chufe to do it yourfelves, or fhould chufe to employ any friend to do it for you.

AND obferve, that in cafe any of the deputies or juftices, or even the lord lieutenant himfelf, fhould offend in any article of

2 G. III. c. 20. f. 51.
Stat. L. viii. 624.
Digeft 57, 58.

the above claufe, you may lay an information againft him, and he is liable to be fined *one hundred pounds*: half of which is to be paid to the profecutor, and half to the poor of the parifh in which the offence was committed; and you may recover it in any of his majefty's courts of record.

IF any deputy or juftice demands and gets from you more than ten pounds, the offence becomes the dirty crime of extortion. Will not the world fay, that the offender finks the character of the generous *Britifh* gentleman, or brave officer, into that of the recruiting ferjeant; and that he forfeits the confidence of his poor countrymen, who look up to him for protection from every wrong? But you may have more fubftantial fatiffaction; you may bring an action againft him, expofe him in a court of juftice, and recover full damages. This may atone for the private injury: but the public wrong is of that moment, as only to be expiated before one of our higheft tribunals; and with all the folemnity of public juftice.

THERE is not one of your fellow-fubjects, let him be ever fo great, that can levy on you a farthing more than the law allows. One of our kings loft his head for trying to raife money without confent of parlement. Surely you have more fpirit than to fuffer any private man to tax you of his own authority? At the fame time you muft pay quietly the ten pounds penalty; but only in cafe you have by law incurred it. But remember, that

this

this payment does not exempt you from ferving again at the end of the three years, or from providing a fubftitute.

THE militia is our great and conftitutional fecurity: it is the intereft of us all to preferve this bulwark of our freedom; but let us all take care that, what was fo ftudioufly intended to be the guardian of our liberties, become not the inftrument of our flavery, in the hands of men who know not the true ufe of power.

IF it was poffible that any deputy or juftice fhould refufe your fubftitutes, and immediately after take thofe very men in the room of other ballotted people, let his fhame be his punifh-ment, for I fear that the act provides none. But as the precife defcription of fit or unfit is quite unfettled, you will, in fuch an inftance, have the comfort of being affured by the very magi-ftrates themfelves, that you never wifhed to affront them by the offer of infufficient people.

IF a poor man is made defperate by the rejection of feveral fit fubftitutes, and by the inability of paying the ten pounds, and afterwards abfconds, he is liable to a more fevere punifh-ment: how far it may exceed the offence, I fubmit to public judgment. At firft the law provided one which feemed equal to the fault, which was a fine of ten pounds, or for want of diftrefs, imprifonment in the common jail, there to live for three months among felons, and ftarve; for I fufpect that he is in a worfe fituation than them, not being comprehended within the king's or county allowance, which the vileft of felons are en-titled to.

THIS claufe was repealed, and the unhappy wretch is, in time of actual fervice, liable to be feized, his name entered on the

roll,

roll, be delivered to an officer of the corps he was ballotted for, torn from his family, hand-cuffed, and marched perhaps two hundred miles acrofs the country; then to ferve three years under perhaps an irritated commander: and fhould he again abfcond, be liable to the infamy of whipping, or to be fhot like the moft profligate deferter. In the name of Heaven! let this claufe be for ever blotted from our ftatutes.

THIS merits the more attention, becaufe nothing is eafier to a mercilefs magiflrate, than to bring a man within this claufe. A poor creature may be able to raife fix or feven pounds to give to the fubftitute whom he has engaged, and yet, with all his endeavours, not be able to raife ten pounds. The magiftrates refufe his fubftitutes, and finding neither money or effects to the value of ten pounds, inftantly convict him of the crime of poverty, and he fuffers accordingly. Or, he may not be a houfeholder, yet be able to pay the ten pounds; but through indignation at the treatment he has received, by the rejection of his fubftitutes, refufes to depofit the money, and having no effects, is in like manner fubject to punifhment.

IN cafe any militia man is difapproved by the commanding officer, after being enrolled, it is lawful for the officer to difcharge him; but he muft give his reafons in writing, and be affifted by two deputy lieutenants: fo attentive, in this inftance, have our law-givers been to the prevention of abufe in the military power! Why have they been fo remifs in the former far more important matter?

PLEASE to obferve, that throughout the militia act, the commanding officer is diftinguifhed from the civil power, or the

deputy

deputy lieutenants and juſtices of the peace. The lord lieutenant alone is permitted to act as colonel: he alone is permitted to unite the civil and military characters, becauſe he can
delegate his powers ſo that his abſence may be diſpenſed with.
In every other inſtance, they are ſo very carefully ſeparated, as
never to appear acting together; except in the inſtance of the
diſcharge of a man, in which they have a ſhort correſpondence.
The law plainly deſigns, that no perſon inferior to the lord lieutenant, ſhould act in both capacities; much leſs to preſide at
the meetings, and brow-beat the deputy lieutenants or juſtices
in the diſcharge of their duty. " A prince, therefore, never
" ſhould give to military men a civil employment: on the
" contrary, they ought to be checked by the civil magiſtrate,
" that the ſame perſons may not have the confidence of the
" people, and the power to abuſe it *."

THE civil power is the ſoul which is to animate the military
machine, and put it in motion. The civil power forms the
men into regiments, or in ſmall counties into companies; aſ-
ſembles men in convenient ſtations, and even poſts to each
company its proper officers.

THE time of training and exerciſing the men, and the place
of rendezvous, is alſo entirely in the power of the lieutenant
and two deputies; or, in the abſence of the lieutenant, in that of
three deputy lieutenants: and the power of embodying the militia is entruſted to the ſame, even in time of actual invaſion, or
in caſe of rebellion.

2 G. III. c. 20. ſ. 28.
Stat. L. viii. 618.
Digeſt 36.

2 G. III. c. 20. ſ. 95.
Stat. L. xiii. 631.
Digeſt 72.

2 G. III. c. 20. ſ. 99.
Stat. L. viii. 632.
Digeſt 74.

2 G. III. c. 20.
ſ. 116.
16 G. III. c. 3. ſ. 1.
Stat. L. xiii. 634.
xii. 431.
Digeſt 98.

* *Monteſquieu.*

M   IN

IN a few words; it does not appear that the commanding officer has scarcely any part to perform till he takes the field: the ballotting, the approving, and the rejecting of volunteers or substitutes, resting entirely in the civil magistrates. The power of the commandant does not commence till, at soonest, the time of enrolling; for within a month after that, he is at liberty to correct the choice of the deputy lieutenants, and to discharge any man whom they have suffered to pass muster, and who is really unfit for service.

2 G. III. c. 20. f. 48.
Stat. L. viii. 623.
Digeſt 102.

GOOD manners, and even prudence, should induce the magistrates to invite any discreet officer of the corps to attend the meeting for accepting of substitutes: or, if the corps is too remote, prudence should urge them to do the same to any fit officer of a neighboring corps, be it regular or militia. They ought not; they cannot be partakers of the power entrusted to the civil magistrates: but they may be usefully consulted on any cases of acceptance, in which the magistrates may have doubts. Every officer is equally a citizen of *Great Britain*; and I dare to say, on this occasion would, in his advice, not forget that most important character.

THE power given to the commandant, of discharging any man he dislikes in one month after enrolling, shews, that it is not supposed he could be present at the ballot, or could have any concern in approving of the substitutes; otherwise, he could not possibly receive improper men one week, in order to discharge them the next.

2 G. III. c. 128.
Stat. L. viii. 637.
Digeſt 6 L.

I SHALL close this suspicion of the probability of the commanding officer's being excluded from all concern in the raising

2   of

of the militia, with this remark, that the overplus of the penalty of ten pounds, if any remains, is to be paid by the deputy lieutenants and juftices to the clerk of the regiment or battalion*, who is to account for it to the colonel or commanding officer; a direction which fufficiently points out the difference of character and diftinction of the department.

MANY of you, in order to eafe yourfelves of expence, have formed clubs, in which every perfon liable to be ballotted fubfcribed a fmall fum, and raifed fufficient to find a fubftitute, in cafe the lot fell on any one of the members. By this means you prevented a heavy load from falling on all fuch, who by reafon of ficknefs, or any other infirmity, were excepted from ferving; but not from the taxes attendant on the militia. This you did freely : and in cafe the lot fell upon any one of you who chofe to ferve, you made ufe of the club-money, and fcorned to put your poor neighbors (for whom you were going to fight) to any more expence than the fupport of your families.

THE law, by a very particular claufe, encourages the ufe of thefe clubs, and as it were, renders optional the ufe of a foregoing claufe; and prevents it from being made burdenfome to any parifhes, except thofe which have been imprudent enough not to form thefe clubs, in eafe to themfelves. But to levy the tax of half the price of a volunteer, as that claufe directs, is a mere wanton exertion of power, in all places where clubs have been eftablifhed.

2 G. III. c. 20. f. 53.
Stat. L. viii. 624.
Digeft 58.

2 G. III. c. 20. f. 47.
19 G. III. c. 72.
Digeft 101.
Stat. L. viii. 623.
xiii. 483.

* By the by, an omiffion in the Digeft.

M 2

HALF

HALF the price of a volunteer has been generally fixed at four guineas, or four and a half: yet I have known, in the very week in which ten or twelve guineas have been prodigally beſtowed on a ſubſtitute, men equally good have been inliſted in the regulars for four; and within five weeks after enrolling, a militia ſubſtitute to ſupply a vacancy has been got by one of the pariſhes for four only.

IN caſe half the price of a volunteer is to be raiſed on the country, you have an indulgence of deferring the payment one whole month. Among other reaſons, is this; it gives time to the overſeers of the poor, who are charged with the payment, to collect the money from their poor brethren, it being well known that many who are thus taxed are worſe off than thoſe for whoſe uſe the money is raiſed. Perhaps almoſt the whole month may be required for the diſtreſſed tenant to get in a little money, notwithſtanding all the trouble and ill-will the overſeer has in diſcharge of his office.

BUT our law-makers had another reaſon for giving you a month's time for the payment; becauſe (as I ſaid before) the commanding officer has power to diſcharge any man he diſ-

The ſame. Sect. 48 in one, 14 in the other.

likes within one month after enrolling, and then no ſuch money is to be paid to that perſon, but to the next choſen by lot in his ſtead. Now it may happen, that if you pay it to the firſt perſon on, or ſoon after the day of enrolling, he may die within the month, or he may be diſcharged, and in the laſt caſe moſt probably may have ſpent the money; in ſo much that the pariſh muſt pay the ſame ſum over again to the next perſon, who is as liable to be diſcharged within a day or two, as the other, and the pariſh

put,

put, without remedy, to freſh expences. Never, therefore, pay the money till the end of the month, and you will be on the ſure ſide, and within the meaning of the law.

You need not fear being put to the expence of maintaining the wives or children of the ſerjeants. In one of your counties, two well-meaning magiſtrates made the trial, but when their order came to the clerk of the peace, who is a very honeſt fellow, he took it, and the matter was totally ſuppreſſed. One ſhould have thought it impoſſible that they could miſtake a non-commiſſion officer for a common man, or not have read, that ſerjeants were appointed from among the common men, and were, on any miſconduct, liable to be reduced to the rank of common men.

2 G. III. c. 20.
ſ. 114.
Digeſt 84.
St. L. viii. 634.
2 G. III. c. 20. ſ. 38.
Digeſt 38
Stat. L. viii. 619.
2 G. III. c. 20. ſ. 39.
Digeſt 39.

THE above is the only perſonal alluſion in this little piece: but I hope I may make free with myſelf, and thus with ſhame and contrition perform my *amende honorable*.

IF any of you are oppreſſed in any manner whatſoever, do not deſpair of relief. Remember you live in a free country, where juſtice is open to the poor as well as the rich. It is not many years ago ſince a great lord, a ſecretary of ſtate, made the ſame miſtake as moſt country juſtices have done, and iſſued a general warrant againſt a private gentleman; who had ſpirit to take the law of his lordſhip, and recovered four thouſand pounds damage. And I remember a cobler near *London*, who went to law with a former king for a foot-path, and caſt his majeſty.

BUT let the law be your laſt reſource. I have not the moſt diſtant thought of ſetting you and the gentry at variance. They

3   are

are bound to give you protection by the duties of humanity; by their duty as magiftrates. They are bound by their oaths " *to do equal juftice to the poor and to the rich, after their cunning* " *wit and power, and after the laws and cuftoms of the realm,* " *and the ftatutes thereof made.*" You are bound to pay to them a manly refpect; for on their integrity, knowlege, and power, YOUR OWN SAFETY DEPENDS. *In our feveral ftations we* are ALL BOUND TO BE PROTECTIONS *one to the other.* If any of them, through heat, or forgetfulnefs of the law, fhould have injured you, apply for redrefs in a private manner. I truft that there are in every *Welfh* county fome worthy gentlemen who will undertake your caufe, and perform the bleffed office of peace-makers. Thofe who may have wronged you, need not be afhamed of making the pooreft of you amends. Reparation of an injury does honor to the offender, and wipes away the offence. The greateft man in *England* may glory in the opportunity.

In diftracted times, fuch as the prefent, petty tyrants are apt to arife, who think they can act fecure in the rage of the ftorm. The watchman is not to be blamed who, in fufpicious feafons, gives the alarm on the fight of the rifing of a diftant duft. I hope, therefore, it will not be thought prefumptuous in me, unbidden, to take the office. Internal impulfes to prevent evils, ought not to be refifted. I am not a firft-rate man among you: but a pygmy armed by juftice goes forth a giant. Within the county in which I am deftined to act, I am in a particular manner bound to befriend you; to befriend you in a good caufe: but if you are wrong, and obftinately wrong, my utmoft endea-vours fhall be ufed to inflict on you every punifhment in the power of the law.

BUT

BUT I hope that peace and mutual confidence will ever reign among us; and that rich and poor will, as is their joint intereſt, endeavour to promote; to the utmoſt of their abilities, RESPECT TO THE LAWS, AND RESPECT TO TRUE LIBERTY.   Such,

My dear countrymen,

is the conſtant wiſh of

Your faſt friend,

Downing,
Nov. 10th, 1781.

THOMAS PENNANT.

APPENDIX,

APPENDIX, N° 3.

A
L E T T E R

FROM A

WELSH FREEHOLDER

TO HIS

REPRESENTATIVE.

1784.

N

ADVERTISEMENT.

A FEW nights ago, my maid brought me a parcel directed to me, which she found flung upon my desk. I have perused it carefully, and find nothing in it but good sound doctrine, and quite agreeable to the laws and usage of the land. I cannot but consider it as a fairy-gift; therefore will not wrong myself so far as not to print it, thinking myself free from blame for turning the penny in an honest way. But at the same time pledge myself to the author (should he hereafter appear) to allow him such a share of profit as shall be adjudged by any two of the trade, with a proper umpire.

J. MONK.

Chester, April 1, 1784.

A

L E T T E R

FROM A

WELSH FREEHOLDER

TO HIS

REPRESENTATIVE.

February 10, 1784.

DEAR SIR,

I AM obliged to you for your favor of *January* 24th, and should have been extremely happy to have received an answer a little more satisfactory. I am most willing to believe that your designs may at this time be pure, that you have no thought to eradicate monarchy, no more than hundreds of great characters had in the beginning of the troubles of the last century, but by the artifices of the popular leaders, they were drawn from violence to violence, till their retreat became impracticable; and when they made the attempt, they were overwhelmed by the tyranny which they unwittingly had helped to establish, and

N 2   which

which foon after totally fubverted the conftitution *. You feem
fhocked at the idea, and are ready to fay with *Hazael*, "Is thy fervant a dog, that he fhould do thefe things?" What is the government of our kingdom, but the wife mixture of King, Lords, and
Commons, each one defigned to be a check on the ill-conduct of
the others: if you deftroy the powers of any one, and the others
fhould unite, you eftablifh the moft abfolute defpotifm, for you
take away the falutary control of the third. Your faying that
the prefent majority is not anti-monarchial is faying nothing; for
if you deprive the King of the power of chufing his own fervants,
or of the other great executive privilege of appointing to places,
you make him merely nominal; an arrant King Log.

Within thefe two months the above has been (as yet happily)
in vain attempted; firft in the endeavour to place in the Commons the difpofition of places in *India* and all its vaft dependencies; fecondly, in the interference of Lord ****, in the difpo-
fal of the dutchy of *Lancafter*; thirdly, in the prefent attempt to
wreft from Majefty the undoubted right of chufing his own minifters: let thefe points be gained by the Commons, and monarchy falls. Have your leaders informed you what government they mean to eftablifh? If prerogative is deftroyed, this
cannot fubfift; for I think the King will never fubmit to be
brought from his prifon at *St. James's*, with the pageantry of
majefty, to give his affent to acts fignified by the pleafure of the
Commons. I truft that we both look with equal horror on a

---

* A fimilar inftance unhappily may be given in our times, when numbers
of the firft national affembly of *France* have been maffacred by the very people,
they labored to free from one of the worft of governments!

King

King without Commons, as Commons without King. The pernicious refolutions of *January* the twelfth are without prece-dent, becaufe unprovoked; the caufe ought to have been of the firft magnitude to have produced fuch effects, which involve all ranks in their deftructive confequence. They are like a fword which paffes undiftinguifhed between innocent and guilty. Your conftituents feel their fhare. All bufinefs is obftructed, and pof-fibly in a few days the whole army is to be let loofe on their fel-low fubjects. What crime has majefty or minifters committed, to bring on them and our country fuch calamities? Has not year after year the King quietly affented to every bill paffed by the two other branches of legiflature for the weakening of his own power? Had he had ill defigns, his own prerogative might have checked the abridgement of his authority. I inftance only the act for taking away the vote of revenue officers, and that for the abolition of the board of trade. The county of **** with great zeal petitioned for the taking away of ufelefs places. Had the inciters of thofe petitions, when they came into power, purfued the defign with the fame fincerity with which they were fupported by the duped counties, they would not have left room to fufpect that the defire of poffeffing the emoluments of Lord *North*'s ad-miniftration was not the chief end by them propofed. Let me name another merit of this reign, for the fecurity of our liberties, in which the Commons had no fhare, I mean the fpontaneous act of the crown which has made the judges independent of the King by giving them their places for life.

To thefe merits of the King, let me oppofe one glaring deme-rit of the Commons. Did not the reprefentatives of the people, in 1716, betray their rights by the feptennial act, and veft in

themfelves

themſelves four years more of power than the conſtitution or their conſtituents ever intended? I will not enter into a diſcuſſion of the eventual good or evil. The charge ought to be ſubject of deep conſideration with electors and elected. But if it was wrong, is not the preſent majority *particeps criminis*, by permitting it to continue unrepealed? But does there not appear the greater probability of its deſign of aſſuming a far longer continuance of its own power, ſhould it not be appalled by the warning voice of the people? I cannot give it a grain of credit for any one act of forbearance, any pretended moderation, ſince the awful ſound begins to roll over its head.

THE King has lately dared to make uſe of his prerogative, in diſmiſſing his late ſervants, for unconſtitutionally trying to divert into another branch of the legiſlature his great prerogative of the diſpoſal of places. Pleaſe to apprehend *that* to be the only part of Mr. *Fox's India* bill to which I make any objection. I ſhould hold chartered rights moſt ſacred; but not ſuch which have affected the lives and properties of millions, in the manner in which the abuſe of power is pretended to have done in our *Indian* empire.

IN place of the miniſtry diſmiſſed, his majeſty has been pleaſed to put at the head of the new one a youth endued, I may ſay, with miraculous abilities; one in whom malice can find as few defects as can be found in human nature. When I had the honor of ſpeaking to you on the ſubject of his virtues, in the ſhort converſation I had with you in your way to town, you ſeemed to have had no objection to him. Has his ſhort adminiſtration been marked by any flagitious deed? Would it not have been fair to have given the man of the King's choice a ſhort trial? Or, is it not becauſe he is the man of the King's choice

choice that the majority of mouths are open againſt him? I hope his virtues are not the object of jealoufy, and that the eloquence of *Themiſtocles* is not to bear down the virtues of *Ariſtides!* furely the majority do not fign the ſhell becauſe they are angry at every body calling *Ariſtides* juſt?

CERTAINLY there are ſtrong contraſts to his character, who unite their force to pull him down. Why ſhould the affairs of the whole nation be ſtopped at the inſtance of ſuch perſons? Could you not ſuffer the buſineſs to go on, with only the proper objections to what was wrong? Surely the taxes might have paſſed, in order to prevent what may poſſibly enſue, univerſal bankruptcy. But moderation muſt not be adopted; it will ſuit neither the views nor intereſts of a ſet of men, whom poverty and ambition have made nearly deſperate. The nonſenſical exploded cry of ſecret influence is for private ends again revived.

EXCUSE me for reminding you (but remind you I muſt) of the declaration you made at the laſt general election, that you would enliſt under no party, follow no ſet of men; the performance is far from impracticable; many illuſtrious characters, who obſerve thoſe excellent rules, exiſt at this very time. Your conſtituents wiſh you to do the ſame. They wiſh to prevale on you to compare your ſentiments with theirs; the ſooner it is done, the leſs will be the violence of the alteration. I firſt ſuggeſted the communication of our ſentiments, and from my model (ſuch as is incloſed) is drawn the declaration which I apprehend has by this time been ſent to you from the gentlemen of ****, with the approbation of many reſpected characters in this end of the county. You need not ſtart at the teſt offered to you. It is not deſigned to bind you to any party,

I   to to any fet of men. It contains only conftitutional fundamentals, fuch as you might fubfcribe without any derogation from your honor. If the name offends, change it to ' inftructions,' and the offence is done away. Why fhould the majority be alarmed at fubfcribing to undeniable duties, who are daily offering to their Sovereign the moft mortifying covenants? This fquea-mifh nicety reminds me of the giant in *Rabelais*, who daily fwal-lowed wind-mills for his breakfaft, and at laft was choaked with a lump of butter before the mouth of a warm oven.

To conclude: there is not a wifh to change our reprefentative, provided he acts confonant to our principles; but none of us ought to give up principle for affection. I truft that your an-fwer will be clear and decided; fo that in fupporting you we fhall fupport the dictates of our own confciences. The great majority of your conftituents are firm friends to the legal prero-gative. They will re-elect you; yet how muft they blufh at their inconfiftency if you take an adverfe part! I have been your friend, and I fhall be forry to withdraw my intereft from you. Excufe me again if I fay, with the fpirit of a freeman, this muft reft in yourfelf. If we differ in fentiments, there ought to be mutual forgivenefs, for it is impoffible to expect from either fide a criminal compliment. I have never yet deceived you; nor will I begin in this late period of life. If we are fo unhappy to difagree in opinion, I will not vote againft you: but cannot vote for you.

I remain, dear Sir,

Your affectionate humble fervant,

A WELSH FREEHOLDER.

APPENDIX,

APPENDIX, N° 4.

TO THE

EDITOR

OF THE

GENERAL EVENING POST.

Havod y lom, Feb. 1781.

SIR,

I HAVE long been very fenfible of the feveral improvements which the military fpirit, fo prevalent in thefe kingdoms, and the frequent incampments, have introduced into the moft diftant counties. At prefent I fhall forbear mentioning the happy effects they have had on the morals of the male part of the community, and confine myfelf to that fex to which we are indebted for every thing which renders life endurable. I was always its fincere admirer; and am happy to find any occafion of pointing out whatfoever may add to their charms, or extend their conquefts.

 I WAS laft fummer in a gentleman's family in the inland part of *England,* with whom I had a long and intimate acquaintance. I happened to reach the place in the dog-days; and finding the

O ladies

ladies fitting in an alcove in their cloth riding habits, inftead of their cool chintzes, I exprefled my fear that I prevented them from taking their morning ride. They affured me, they did not mean to ftir out; and one of them, clapping on a vaft hat with a cockade, declared fhe would only go for her work, and fit down for the reft of the morning. On turning round, how was my rufticity furprized to fee her hair clubbed behind! another gave me an opportunity of feeing a whifking queue; and a third a greafy braid, hanging down and dabbing the fhining cape!

AFTER the morning was far fpent, Mifs *Dorothy* (for, in imitation of the quality, there are now no fuch things as *Dollies, Mollies,* and *Betties)* with a great yawn flung her arms over her head, and her legs a yard before her, and informed us, it was dreffing time: then pulling her watch out of (I believe) a tight leathern breeches, acquainted us, that it was half paft two; and returned it to its place with a moft officer-like air.

I SAW the countenance of my good old friend change. As foon as the ladies had left the place, he gave vent to his difcontent in the following terms: " My dear *Jack,*" fays he, " what an
" alteration is there in the manners of this houfe fince I laft had
" the happinefs of your company! A curfed vifit to *Coxheath*
" hath infected my poor girls to a degree that gives me the
" keeneft concern. The chafte and elegant drefs, which was
" once their characteriftic, is now converted into what you have
" juft feen. Female delicacy is changed into mafculine cou-
" rage, and as much of the garb affumed as at firft view almoft
" leaves the difference of fex undiftinguifhable. The manly
" habit is put on with the morning, and, as you will fee pre-
" fently, only changed for another of the fame kind. The

a   " watch

" watch too has alfo quitted its modeft ftation, and the fair
" wearer, inftead of confulting the hour with the former grace-
" ful recline of the head, now boldly lugs out the oracle, and
" afterwards thrufts it—the lord knows where! My niece *Eli-*
" *zabeth,* in defence of this new mode, fays, that its motions
" are confiderably altered fince it had experienced a new fitua-
" tion. No wonder, fince it had quitted the temperate for the
" torrid zone. A long ftring, with all the mafculine load of
" feals, &c. now affectedly hangs down the center of the fair
" frame; fometimes it is formed of hair, ending with a ftrange
" fringe of the fame. A celebrated antiquarian affured me
" that this was the true love-lock. And a wicked rogue added,
" that it was an excellent conductor of amorous ideas to our
" fex, a remembrancer to our flack youth, and, like a ftrange
" peculiarity in the drefs of the ladies of *Siam,* which ferves as
" a whet to the depraved appetites of their copper-coloured
" gallants. Inftead of ———" I could no longer bear his prof-
ing, fo diverted the difcourfe : but not without giving internal
affent to part of his reflections, even tinctured as they were by
the foolifh prejudices of old age. Laudable as a due attention
is to fafhion in young people, yet I was brought to confefs that
there were indecencies in thofe of the prefent year, which are
the difguft of the grave, the fcoff of the licentious ; are marks
of a light mind, or bring under fufpicion of levity the pureft
heart, which thoughtlefsly adopts the unfuitable manners or habit of our fex.

I am,

Your humble fervant,

C A M B E R.

O 2   APPENDIX,

APPENDIX, N° 5.

MISCELLANIES.

Old Bond-ſtreet, Auguſt 10, 1774.

SIR,

I WAS the other day in a coffee-houſe filled with (not the firſt rate) company of this great town, where I long ſate indig- nant at the topic which employed every tongue. I could have born with patience the common ſubjects of politics, the mere offspring of ignorance and rancour; but when I found their licentious mouths filled with the moſt infamous inferences, drawn from the unhappy conduct of a lady not leſs eminent for her rank than her beauty, I flung down my penny in a rage, and retired to my apartments full of reflections on ſome events unfortunately at this time too well known.

THE love of fame in either ſex is a principle implanted in us for the moſt noble purpoſes, and is often of itſelf productive of the moſt important and generous effects. The character of the tender part of the creation confines them to a narrower ſphere of action: but their duties are not leſs conſequential than thoſe of our ſex, which make more eclat; and are attended with all the rewards that public merit can claim. If it is the lot of the fair to become wives and parents, a virtuous diſcharge of the duties of thoſe relations ſhould be the ſum of their ambition. But if

it

it be their fortune to remain single, an equal fame will attend them by that delicacy and eafe of behaviour towards the men, which form the genuine characteriftics of virtue. If once this honeft fpecies of ambition forfakes them, and an anxiety after foreign admiration feizes them, they become the mark of every profligate wretch, or fluttering infect; who may perhaps finge his wings, but at the fame time is fure to impair the brightnefs of the luminary. Every foft look, and every little levity, be-comes encouragement; and the enduring of one free action is fure to lay a foundation for another. The man of gallantry prefumes on appearances, miftakes culpable vanity for vitious inclinations, and in the end, moft defervedly, fuffers for his er-ror: he is difgracefully driven from the chateau by infulting do-meftics; or fuffers ftill more marked mortifications, at the com-mand of the infulted fair. She diftreffes her poor hufband with her complaints: fhe wonders at the fellow's impudence. Alas! what can the unhappy fpoufe reply, but what muft add to her and his own mifery? He may (but it is more likely his fufpicions may take an unhappy turn at the fame time) he may, I fay, allow her to be innocent at the bottom; but he will re-proach her with having given the gallant every reafon to expect an eafy conqueft: he may alfo unjuftly conceive a jealoufy that there may have been, or that there ftill may be, moments when poor virtue may be caught napping, and the fum of female dif-honour effected. His peace of mind is gone; and mutual wretchednefs becomes the price of the mere moments of levity, or the love of tranfient admiration.

EVERY attempt for that purpofe becomes criminal; fince the conclufion is often as uncertain as it is unexpected. To call

aloud

aloud in public to men of gaiety; to fuffer an unmeaning whif-
per; or to retire to a remote feat; are acts which bring with
them the caufe of the moft cruel fcandal.   In private company
to force yourfelf at table almoft on the lap of your favorite; to
rivet your eye on his; to catch frequently at his hand, or every
now and then to place your's on his knee; or mutually to dan-
gle your hands over the elbow chair, that they may come un-
perceived in contact, give as great difguft to the company as
they do folid injury to the reputation of the fair offender, whether fhe is married or whether fhe is fingle.   If the object of
attraction be a married man, how aggravated is the offence:
how pitiable is the fituation of the poor injured fpoufe! And
yet this fpecies of conduct is very frequent, but never is paffed
unnoticed: the encouragement either brings unhappinefs on the
thoughtlefs fair; or bufy fcandal fixes on her an indelible blot:
a cruel penalty! yet fhe falls unpitied, as it is brought on her by
a criminal or infolent inattention to appearances.

C A M B E R.

A P P E N D I X,

APPENDIX, N° 6.

MISCELLANIES.

FLINTSHIRE PETITION.

THE clamors raifed in the year 1779, and the apparent difcontents grew to fuch a height, that I thought it prudent that the county of *Flint* fhould add its weight to the petition, fo that by prevaling on government to leffen every unneceffary burden, the minds of the people might be eafed, and all ill confequences prevented, for civil war was almoft threatened. I at all times profeffed my abhorrence of committees and affociations. Sir *Roger Moftyn* advifed me to write to fome of our principal gentlemen to inform them of the terms on which I undertook to excite the county to petition, fo that they might decline fubfcribing to the requifition, in cafe they difliked my plan: or if they did fign it, fupport me to its full extent. None to whom I wrote appeared at the meeting. Mr. *Yonge*, one of the friends to whom I wrote, difliked the petition, and declined figning the requifition. Sir *Stephen Glynn*, bart. and *Philip Lloyd Fletcher*, efq. approved my plan, and promifed it every fupport, and to adhere to the very letter of it. Mr. *Fletcher* alfo

fent

fent my letter along with the requifition to the gentlemen of his neighborhood, that they might not miftake the terms on which they were to fign. I came to the meeting in a full reliance on the faith of my countrymen: but the dean of St. *Afaph*, burning after the glory of chairman of a committee, and backed by friends he brought with him, propofed a committee, and carried his point.

I DID intend to deliver the following fpeech, but my fpirits failed me.

" BEING totally unufed to fpeak in public, I beg leave, in faultering words, to lay before you the motives which induced me to promote this meeting.

" THE diftreffes of the times are too evident to admit of contradiction. To have recourfe to any legal method of alleviating our fufferings is extremely natural. The only one which prefents itfelf is, ' by petition to the high court of parliament,' a privilege preferved to us by the BILL of RIGHTS, and which can never be exerted with more propriety than at prefent, provided refpect and moderation attend it.

" IT is faid by an able fpeaker on the fide of oppofition, ' that 300,000 l. may be annually faved by retrenching the emoluments of offices, and abolifhing the long train of ufelefs placemen and penfioners.' As I make no doubt but this gentleman can fupport his affertion, let me obferve, that the above fum will, at the rate of five per cent. pay the intereft of more than fix millions of money; and of courfe, in the next year, eafe the all-fupporting landlord and tenant from a burden equal to that fum.

" THIS alone, in the neceffitous ftate of our country (which

from

from the nature of its trade fuffers more in proportion than others) ought to determine us to make ufe of the propofed method of relief, leaving it to the wifdom of parlement feverely to fcrutinize into the nature of our grievances, and to rectify every one which may be difcovered to exift. It is juft to enquire before we condemn. Let the accufed, if guilty, fuffer the penalty of their neglect; if innocent, acquitted with honor. But let the minds of the people be eafed, by a proper enquiry into the foundation of the national difcontent.

" THAT invaluable compilation the *Red-book* * furnifhes me with a very fingular inftance of a place of little moment, attended with a high falary. I cannot but fmile at feeing the reprefentative of one of our firft cities, and one of the lords commiffioners of the admiralty, unite with that important charge the poft of *letter-carrier* to the court, with the lavifh falary of 730*l.* a year. The duty might perhaps be performed (if any there is) by a lefs refpectable perfon, for 2*s.* 6*d.* a day; and I will not pay a very worthy gentleman fo bad a compliment, as to fuppofe, that his principles will be in the left altered by being free from fuch a degrading office.

" MANY fimilar inftances may probably be found, all worthy of being lopped off: but let me do the times the juftice to fay, that few of them are of recent formation; they are the antient marks of regal ftate, created in profperous days. In the progrefs of enquiry, it will be worthy to remark the periods when they ceafed to be ornaments to the crown, and became the inftruments of corruption.

* Edition 1779, pages 39, 122.

P "THE

" The affair of contracts is beyond my power to speak to.
It will be our wish that parlement would guard against the
abuse of them, and examine whether the princely state in which
our contractors live, arises from any thing beyond the fair profits
of their business.

" In attending to the report of any party on that subject, or
any other, we ought to take particular care not to be too credu-
lous.   I say this because of the alarm that has (I trust causelessly)
arisen among *us*, of a design of altering the courts of justice in
the principality in a manner grievous to the *Welch*: let us wait
with patience till the honorable member has laid open his design ;
and if it is then found to be a grievance, let us resist it with
the same firmness as we did the treasury warrant.   I hereby declare, not only in my own name, but in that of many respectable
friends, great and small freeholders, that we do not, by signing
the petition before us, exclude ourselves from seeking legal re-
dress from any innovation, which may appear unjust and burden-
some, let it come from any quarter whatsoever.

" The body of us petitioners consists of a stupendous multitude of persons, actuated with very different objects.   I believe
I may say with confidence, that there is not an individual in this
assembly who has not the most laudable motives in view, ab-
stracted from every party spirit whatsoever.

" There are many very worthy and well-meaning gentlemen
who think we have chosen an improper season for petitioning,
amidst the rage of war.   But let it be observed, that the strength
of government consists in the variety of its resources, and if we
are able to point out a most important one, we rather accelerate
than impede its motion.   In the peaceable times to refuse sup-

*

plies.

plies would be a proper infult to an obftinate minifter; but NOW! in the moment of RETURNING VICTORY *! it would be a meafure fraught with certain danger and poffible parricide.

" I AM not of confequence enough to trouble you with profeffions, efpecially as I have no other object than to add my mite to ferve my country; I fhall only detain you, while I acquaint you with the fteps I took after I had formed the refolution of exciting the county to affemble on this occafion. I drew up the requifition to the fheriff: I fent it, accompanied with a letter, expreffive of my fentiments, to the three worthy gentlemen before mentioned. That I did not fend it to more, was for want of time, not of refpect. From my letter, and from the fubftance of a petition I fent with it, they might judge of the utmoft limits of my intentions, that in cafe they difapproved of my defign, they might decline fubfcribing to my requifition. It was returned to me, figned by an ample number, to whom I beg leave to return thanks for the compliment they were pleafed to pay me.

" I objected in that letter, and I do now in the ftrongeft manner object, to all party-affociations, and for myfelf decline the honors of committee-man.

" THE former may end in combinations injurious to our peace, and perhaps fatal at the laft to thofe who embark in them. We MUST not fend our reprefentative to the houfe with our prayer in one hand, and a dagger in the other. We MUST not attempt to intimidate the houfe from freedom of debate, at the time we are ftriving to wreft from men of power the peftilential baits

* Lord *Rodney's* defeat of the *Spanish* fleet, *January* 16th, 1780.

of

of corruption: we MUST not wound when we wiſh to amend
the diſeaſes of our conſtitution: we MUST be conſiſtent with
ourſelves.   The parlement will ſuffer a civil death in leſs
than a twelvemonth; it will be the fault of the people if they
chuſe another compoſed of members with whom they are at
preſent ſo diſcontented.   They will, when that period arrives,
have an opportunity of legally rejecting thoſe candidates whom
they diſapprove, and ſelecting thoſe only worthy of their confidence."

My mention of petitioning with a dagger in one hand gave
great offence; but I thought myſelf vindicated by the indecent
language of ſome of the petitioners, of which the following is a
ſpecimen.

" Such were the people who agreed to the petition on which
" I now lean.   Oeconomy in the expenditure of the public
" money is all they aſk.   Will any man vote for rejecting ſo
" modeſt, ſo reaſonable a requeſt? I hope not.   Will any man
" vote that this petition be not brought up? No man, I truſt,
" will dare do it.   The miniſter will not dare do it, becauſe he
" knows he ought not to dare it.   But there is another thing
" alſo which he ought not to dare; and that is, to attempt to
" defeat the object of it.   If the miniſter is ſo inclined, with the
" turn of his finger he may deſtroy it: but let him beware how
" he directs his influence againſt it.   Let me adviſe him to be-
" ware how he inſtitutes an enquiry into the merits of the peti-
" tion: it ſpeaks for itſelf; and the petitioners will look upon
" ſuch an enquiry as a mockery, as a parlementary or mini-
" ſterial trick to put an indirect negative upon their petition.
" When they met to draw it up they were unarmed; they had

2   " neither

" neither mufkets nor ftaves; but if you mock them, they will
" ——————— I'll leave blanks for the fagacity of the houfe
" to fill up."

Lord *Ongly* reprobated the idea of threats, notwithstanding he was a petitioner, and voted in this inftance with the minority.

" Lord *Ongly* reprobated, in fevere terms, the connection
" that fubfifted between the petition and county affociations.
" Threats had been hinted, and more than hinted, if the prayer
" of this and of other fimilar petitions fhould be rejected. This
" alone, in his lordfhip's opinion, was fufficient to damn the
" petition. It puts me in mind, faid he, of the man who went
" about robbing, under pretence of felling rabbits. He held
" out the rabbits in one hand, and a piftol in the other, and
" very civilly afked thofe he chanced to meet, whether they
" chofe to buy any rabbits. Such is the conduct of the peti-
" tioners in the different counties; a conduct, which, if it is
" not checked in the bud, may be productive of the moft fatal
" confequences to the liberty and happinefs of this country."

The clamor continued. I was attacked in the papers, and I put an end to the war by the following anfwer.

Downing, March 3, 1780.

Mr. Monk,

PERMIT me, through your paper, to thank the gentleman-like freeholder of the county of *Flint*, for his explanation of the myfterious word *Affociations*. I fo fully approve the end which he intends, that (provided he would fecure them from

proceeding

proceeding any farther) I do declare, that had I not feen the name of our reprefentative in the glorious lift of the lamented minority of 186, I would, at the next general election, have voted, but not affociated, againft him.   Now! let the gloomy idea of the word, and the *air-drawn dagger*, vanifh.   But I muft remain mafter of myfelf.   Neither KING nor People fhall have the fole keeping of my political confcience.   Free was I born; free have I lived; and free, I truft, will die

THOMAS PENNANT.

APPENDIX,

APPENDIX, N° 7.

A

LETTER

TO A

MEMBER OF PARLIAMENT,

ON

MAIL-COACHES.

FACIT INDIGNATIO!

By THOMAS PENNANT, Efq.

1792.

A

L E T T E R, &c.

DEAR SIR,

I AM much obliged to you for your favor of the 5th inftant. I pay fuch deference to your opinion, that I entirely lay afide all thoughts of troubling your honorable houfe with the affair of repealing the act of exemption of mail-coaches from the payment of tolls. I would avoid every adventure which does not promife fuccefs, and fhould be much mortified to be unhorfed and laid fprawling on the *arena* of *St. Stephen's*.

YET I fhall be extremely forry that any member of your houfe fhould, through any quicknefs of mifapprehenfion, wilful or natural, imagine me to be fo wild as to think of an attempt that was not founded on reafonable and honeft principles.

I AM fenfible that the exemption of the mails from the payment of tolls commenced very early: I think, firft by an act of *William* and *Mary*, which was afterwards repeated in feveral others, till it was oppreffively confirmed by that of the 25th *Geo*. III.

THE moft fecond-fighted of your houfe could never have forefeen that the ufage of the fingle horfe and poft-boy, afterwards in many parts converted into the light mail-cart drawn by one horfe, would be fuperfeded by a *royal* carriage drawn by four horfes, and filled by paffengers, who before rode in the common ftages, and contributed to fupport the roads which they paffed over. This unfortunate change proceeded

Q   from

from an extent of prerogative, repined at only when perverted to the injury of the fubject; as this moft inconteftably muft be allowed to have done.

UNDER the fanction of the firft act, turnpike gates were erected, and immenfe fums of money lent on the national faith. For a long time the fecurity was efteemed good; and in. *Wales*, where five per cent. was given, people at firft were happy to place their money on mortgages they imagined fo fafe. The transfer was then eafy, and the public refted perfectly content. The commiffioners did their duty fully: they laid out the money to the beft advantage; nor did they defift till the lowering of the tolls, by the fatal change of the mode of conveyance, had taken place.

I WILL exemplify the hardfhips only in the country I live. Other places equally remote from the capital muft come in for their fhare of the grievance: but they will fall under the common defcription.

BEFORE the inftitution of mail-coaches, two ftage-coaches ran through the county of *Flint*. And, were it not for an evafion, the change of horfes between gate and gate in the *Moftyn* diftrict, one of the diftricts principally aggrieved, each would have paid forty pounds a year. This unhappily was left unguarded in the act. By the help of that evafion both together only paid that fum: and even that fum, had we not been deprived of it, would have enabled us to take up 800*l.* more; and given us the power of repairing every part of the road which was not unexceptionably good.

MANY parts may have been allowed to have been indifferent; but they were adequate to the ufes of the country, not only for

6

the

the use of the farmers and the carriers, but also for the luxury of carriages.

In this state they were found at the introduction of mail-coaches. These soon occasioned the suppression of the common stages, and deprived us at once of forty pounds of annual income. In the year 1789, a person was sent from the general post-office to survey the roads. From his report, and by the orders of the post-office, indictments were preferred at the great sessions at *Mold*, against the whole extent of road in the narrow but long county of *Flint*. In some instances, I fear the grand jury made a strain of their consciences in finding the bills; for some of the indicted places were in most admirable repair. But we were unwilling to obstruct any thing that tended to promote the public good.

Fines to the amount of 1200 *l.* were imposed on the several townships, many of which were very small, and the inhabitants composed of small farmers, and laborers, poor and distressed to the highest degree.

Two of these townships had a great extent of road, and only a few labourers, and a few miserable teams, to perform their statute duty. One of these townships, terrified with the prospect of ruin, by the execution of the *summum jus*, performed twenty-two days duty upon the road. The other township had only a single farmer living in it, who performed a duty of twenty-eight days.

The vast expences which the commissioners had been at in the repairs of the roads, had almost exhausted the credit, in some totally; so that at present 50 *l.* cannot be obtained for 400 *l.* worth of our parchment securities.

Q 2 AT

At this period I was moved with compaffion at the complaint and diftreffes of the poor. This induced me to write my circular letter to the feveral grand juries of *England* and *Wales*, in order to induce them to unite in a common caufe. I blufh at my want of fuccefs, refulting from either ignorance of, or indifference to, the firft principles of fecurity of property. I was fimple enough to think that the juftice of the caufe would have infured an approbation of my plan. Inftead of that, I am told, that in fome places it was even treated with rudenefs and contempt. I ventured even to write to two gentlemen with whom I was not perfonally acquainted: they never paid the left attention to my letter: they forgot my character, and they forgot their own.

I took the liberty of getting my circular letter conveyed to a third gentleman high in office, with whom I was acquainted. It was returned with (written on a corner of it) " Mr. *Pennant* is in the wrong, and I will have no concern in the affair." The gentleman may be politically right; but I am confident that Mr. *Pennant* is not morally wrong.

There has certainly been a ftrong mifapprehenfion of my meaning. I did not intend the abolition of mail-coaches: they have their objections; whether we confider the barbarity with which the poor horfes are treated, or the very frequent deftruction of the paffengers—our old *Jehus* may have flain their thoufands; our modern, their tens of thoufands. I only wifhed that they might not prove oppreffive to many of our counties, by caufes I have before mentioned. True it is, that, in my firft circular letter, I did moft rafhly and unadvifedly hint, that they might, without injury, be converted into the mail-cart.

The

The gentlemen of *Somerfetſhire*, who, I muſt confeſs, did admit that ſomething ſhould be done for us, very juſtly fired on the idea of ſending their *Theſpis* again into his cart. A worthy friend of mine of that county warmly but kindly expoſtulated with me on the ſubject: but I hope this my declaration of repentance will be admitted, and atone for my error.

THE grand juries of *Cheſhire, Berkſhire, Monmouthſhire*, and thoſe of *North Wales*, united in the ſupport of my deſign. The reſt of the counties proved to me the truth of the remark of *Swift*, " That he never knew any perſon who did not bear the " misfortunes of another perfectly like a Chriſtian !"

FAR the majority of the roads in *England* have great revenues, ariſing from the multitude of ſtage-coaches that keep their ground in defiance of mails. Our ſtages are obliged to deſiſt from travelling, and give the former a moſt unjuſt and oppreſſive monopoly. The counties intereſted in them feel not our unhappineſs, and want generoſity to contribute to the alleviation of the diſtreſſes we ſuffer.

WE ſhould have made a claim on the juſtice of the houſe, had we had the moſt diſtant proſpect of ſucceſs. We are now in the caſe of creditors defrauded by the ſuperior cunning of an artful debtor. Had an individual received an adequate mortgage on his eſtate, and had afterwards the dexterity to leſſen the income, what name would he have deſerved? The higheſt term of reproach; but ſuch a one that could never be applied the moſt remotely to any member of your honorable houſe.

THIS affair has never yet been ſeriouſly conſidered. Good men, I truſt, will now awake as from a ſleep; and ſtand amazed and confuſed at the ſad deluſion they diſcovered that they had labored under. Favourite ſyſtems run away with mankind,

and

and totally annihilate all attention to the inconveniences they occasion. The act was obtained late in the sessions, hurried through a very thin house, and with the slightest opposition. The legislature obliges a certain time of notice to be given before the introduction of a common turnpike bill. Let me ask, Should not at left the interval of a session have been given for the discussion of so strange and unequal a taxation?

WHAT, may I ask, could make the individual liable to censure; and the actions of the collective body be passed over without blame? Either the numbers defend, or some dæmon, like the ghostly father of *Charles* I. has whispered in your ears, Have a double conscience! one that is to make you consult the plain dictates of honesty: the other telling you to support some fancied public good, at the expence of a certain number of persons, who, in times not very remote, had trusted their money to the security of the public faith.

OR may you not hold the same doctrine as the nuns in *Tristram Shandy*; that the divisibility of sin may enable you to fritter it away into almost nothing?—You certainly have the advantage. The nuns were but two, you are five hundred and fifty-two to bear the feather-weight of the wrong decision, you had most unwarily been induced to make.

LET me now ask, Are there no instances of repeal of acts on far less important occasions? I well recollect two. The first is the *Jew Act*, which had in fact no consequences to be feared, religious or political. The other was the cyder tax, esteemed like ours a partial grievance; and yet its overthrow was easily effected. I reflect on these two acts repealed without cause, and on our oppressions continued in defiance of every principle of justice.

SINCE

SINCE your honorable houſe was determined to weaken our ſecurities, ought it not to have firſt paid off every turnpike mortgage? and then you might have had full liberty of doing what you pleaſed with the income of the gates.

I BEG leave to lay before you a caſe in which your houſe once ſhewed a moſt ſcrupulous attention to the rights of creditors. That was by the repeal of a clauſe in the *Kingſland* turnpike act. Part of it leads from *Shoreditch* to *Ware,* and this part was croſſed by the *Newmarket* road, and tolls were taken by the commiſſioners of the *Ware* road, from all travellers to and from that ſeminary of virtue, merely for croſſing the road. On the renewing of the *Kingſland* turnpike act, the *Newmarket* people inſiſted that they ſhould paſs free of tolls. A clauſe was inſerted in the new act for that purpoſe, and the croſs-gates were pulled down. The creditors of the *Kingſland* turnpike petitioned to the houſe of commons for redreſs; they ſucceeded, and the croſs-gates were again erected, and the tolls taken till the whole of the creditors were paid.

I IMAGINE

I IMAGINE that there is not a member of the houfe who has not acted as a commiffioner of the turnpikes. Let me requeft him to call to mind, whether he has not in that character, or in the character of a magiftrate, treated with a harfh feverity the delinquent who, through poverty, has defrauded the gate of nine-pence. What pleas of confcience have not the commiffioners urged for maintaining the interefts of the gates, and difcharging their truft like men of honor? Is there not a *Lethean* atmo-fphere in the chapel of *St. Stephen*, fo fuddenly to efface all me-mory of tranfactions in the common air of the world? I truft that there is: otherwife the individual who, in one place and in one character, had been fo ftrenuous to fave a poor nine-pence, fhould in another place, and in another character, vote as a per-quifite to the comptroller-general of the poft-office, an exemp-tion of the mails from toll, a fum amounting to not lefs than 90,000 *l.* a year, on which he has a moft confiderable poundage, befides fome very good pickings from other articles. This I am affured of by a worthy member of your houfe. I think his falary is but 1500 *l.* per ann. What a monftrous quantity of fack is allowed to his halfpennyworth of bread!

So liberally fupplied as the comptroller has been with the means, cannot fomething be deducted to relieve our complaint? If the honorable houfe does not choofe this mode, a fmall, a very fmall tax on the paffengers, and on the immenfe fums got by the carriage of parcels, would compenfate for the lofs of exemption of tolls. The rich *Englifh* diftricts would be above taking advantage of this diminution of revenue to the comp-troller-general. It is only for the poor *Welch* diftricts, and a few others like circumftanced, for which it is humbly afked.

I HAVE

I HAVE a refpect for the plan of the mail-coaches, and for the inventor; but I never could think of applying to him as the *nizam al muluc*, the regulator of the pofting-empire. There ought not to be in our conftitution fuch a monfter as a comptroller uncontrollable by his legiflature, or his fuperiors in office: legiflature muft now fee its imprudence in permitting a latitude of fo dangerous a nature. I, an individual, never could bear the thought: I looked for redrefs to the poft-mafter general, or to the three eftates of the kingdom.

I FEAR too great a veneration has been paid to this new-created office, and mode of conveying the mail. I always wifh to pay every individual and every office a due refpect; but in this cafe I muft preferve the independent and ufeful man, and endeavour to correct every abufe that falls within my fphere as a provincial magiftrate. What I am going to fay may be deemed foreign to a legiflative friend; yet as it may prove ufeful to many who behold thefe new vehicles with a kind of veneration, I fhall mention an affair which happened in our county in the laft autumn. Let me premife, that thofe protectors of the mail, the guards, relying on the name of royalty, had in the courfe of the *Irifh* road through *North Wales*, committed great exceffes. One, on a trifling quarrel, fhot dead a poor old gate-keeper: a coroner's jury was huddled up; and, in defiance of the tears of the widow, no judicial notice has been taken of the affair to this very day. In *Anglefey*, another of thefe guards difcharged his piftol wantonly in the face of a chaife horfe, drawing his mafter, the Rev. *John Bulkely*, who was flung out, and died either on the fpot or foon after. Thefe guards fhoot at dogs, hogs, fheep and poultry,

R

as they pafs the road, and even in towns, to the great terror and danger of the inhabitants. I determined to put a ftop to thefe exceffes, and foon had an opportunity.

A NEIGHBORING gate-keeper laid before me a complaint, that one of the guards had threatened to blow his brains out; and had actually fhot a dog that had offended him by his barking. I iffued out my warrant, had the guard feized, and brought before me. He was a man who, for his great beauty and elegant per-fon, was called the *Prince* of *Wales*. I did not hefitate to play the Judge *Gafcoigne*; but from the goodnefs of his appearance, and the propriety of his behaviour, I did not go quite the length that famous magiftrate did. I took bail for his appearance at our quarter feffions. He appeared before us, when, by the permiffion of the chairman, I took the lead in fpeaking. I reprefented to the audience, that the guards were intrufted with arms merely for the protection of the mail and the paffengers, not for the terror of his Majefty's fubjects; that a mail-coach was no fanctuary; that the bailiff might drag the debtor out of it; the conftable, the felon; the excifeman might rummage it for contraband goods, and that with as little ceremony as if it had been a higler's cart. I far-ther added, had the driver been the offender, as the guard was, he fhould have been taken into cuftody, and the poft-mafter of the diftrict left to provide another to convey the mail to the next ftage. The behaviour of the delinquent was fo becoming his fituation, that by the leave of the court I difmiffed the offender with fuch a reprimand as became the high ftation of a *Britifh* juftice of the peace: an office in dignity and conftitutional utility inferior to none in the land. Young men of the age, early initiate yourfelves into that great character!

8

I BEG

I BEG pardon for detaining you fo long, but fo much I thought was due to myfelf and to the public. A few papers I have fubjoined will fling fome farther light on the fubject, as well as on my proceedings from the beginning. I remain, with much regard,

DEAR SIR,
Your faithful and
affectionate humble fervant,
THOMAS PENNANT.

George-ftreet, Hanover-fquare,
March 31, 1792.

Downing, Feb. 18, 1793.

P. S. Notwithftanding the lenity fhewn to the mail guard, the drivers of the coaches continue their infolencies. It has been a common practice with them to divert themfelves with flinging out their lafhes at harmlefs paffengers by way of fun. Very lately one of thefe wretches fucceeded fo well as to twift his lafh round a poor fellow's neck in the parifh I live. He dragged the man under the wheels, by which one of his arms was broken. If ample fatisfaction is not made, an action fhall be commenced againft the proprietors of the coach, who are cerrainly anfwerable for the mifconduct of their people.

LETTER

LETTER to *Thomas Williams*, Efq. of *Llanidan*, Member for the Borough of *Marlow*.

DEAR SIR, *Downing, Oct. 18, 1791.*

I AM much indebted to you for your late favor, with an official letter inclofed. I have no kind of doubt but that the comptroller general will, on cool re-confideration of his defign of altering the courfe of the *Irifh* mail, be induced to lay it totally afide. He will admit the importance of the county of *Chefter* in its ancient ftaple of the cheefe, on which our fleets and armies fo greatly depend. The city itfelf (if I may judge by the frequent advertifements) is about to enter deeply on the fuftian manufacture. The great remittances of taxes from the county, and from great part of *North Wales*, and the remittances to and from *Ireland*, and thofe occafioned by the great biennial linen fairs, muft be flung into the fcale.

THE port of *Park-Gate* has of late years rifen into much confequence. It at prefent maintains four ftout pacquets, which uninterruptedly ply between that port and *Dublin*. The correfpondencies of the numbers of paffengers embarking or difembarking, and the great remittances through this channel, are of no fmall moment, and of great general concern.

THE county of *Flint* (little as it is of itfelf), thanks to you and other companies, fettling among us, is now rifing into an amazing ftate of opulence: few perhaps can rival it. Our an-

cient

cient lead trade was always confiderable; but by the introduction
of the copper and cotton bufinefs, *Holywell*, its environs, and
their dependencies, may boaft of commercial property, probably to the amount of a million fterling.

I HAVE always confidered Mr. *Palmer*'s plan as ufeful to his
country, and an honor to himfelf, except in one article. I can
never fuppofe that he will perfift in deviating from the utility of
his fcheme, by diverting the mail from fuch a country as I have
defcribed. *Shrewfbury* has already its mail; after *Ofweftry* is paft,
the greateft part of the road to *Conwy* is mountainous, poor, and
half depopulated.

IT gives me concern to find our interefts clafh with thofe of the
county of *Salop*. I muft allow the excellency of the great ftaples
of its capital, brawn and rich cakes; but ftill we have the balance
in our favor; for on the moft exact and impartial calculation, I
do not find that at prefent the annual confumption (of both together) can poffibly exceed the fum of 152,341 *l.* 16*s.* 9 *d.*

THE exceptionable article I allude to is the exemption of the
mail-coaches from tolls. This falls heavy on the leffer diftricts:
poffibly we might have endured even that, had we not been infulted with indictments, and compelled to repairs beyond the real
wants of the country. That is now over; we only wifh the
reftoration of our loft tolls, to enable us to fupport the roads in
the prefent ftate, and to take away all future grounds of complaint from every quarter. This will induce me to perfift in my
defign of applying to parlement for redrefs of the grievance that
affects the gates from *Chefter* to *Conwy*, let the rich *Englifh* diftricts
take what fhare they pleafe in their own concerns. There is
one difficulty in *Flintfhire* in refpect to the road itfelf—I mean

Rhiallt

Rhiallt Hill; the alteration is beyond the power of the poor parifh it lies in, and beyond the power of the poor *Moftyn* diftrict to effect.   Poffibly the improvement may coft from 300*l.* to 400*l.* a fum adequate to the eftimate has been raifed by the voluntary fubfcription of the neighboring gentlemen: and the place moftly complained of, has been moft nobly improved, at the expence of 221*l.* 18*s.* 3*d.* I wifh a fmall fum might be got from parlement, for that and the relief of a few other poor townfhips. I cannot bear to drive over roads fmoothed by the bread of the poor peafantry.   If the mail will be permanent, I will cheerfully fubfcribe fifty guineas towards that improvement.   I fhall conclude with faying, that a fmall addition to the fare of paffengers between *Chefter* and *Conwy*, will indemnify the coach from the lofs by toll.   Let Mr. *Palmer*, who cannot but be fertile in expedients, confider of the matter.   My earneft wifh is to have harmony reftored, and the ftrongeft mutual efforts made for the general good.

I am,

DEAR SIR,

Your moft obedient humble fervant,

THOMAS PENNANT.

A LET-

A LETTER to the worſhipful *Peter Broſter*, Eſq.
Mayor of *Cheſter*.

Downing, January 23, 1792.

S I R,

ON *Thurſday* two letters were laid by Mr. *Smalley* before the commiſſioners of the *Flint, Holywell,* and *Moſtyn* diſtricts, ſigned D. *Smith,* and G. *Boulton;* in which our attention was requeſted to the repair of the roads which lay in our county in the courſe of the mail. It falls to my lot to deſire you to communicate to your reſpectable corporation, what the commiſſioners have done, and what they intend to do of their own proper motions, not from the fear of any of the very unbecoming menaces ſent forth.

On the road from *Holywell* to the extremity of the diſtrict (which is called the *Flint*), has been laid out, within two years, 953*l.* in the ſpace of five miles: great part of which, long before the indictments, was in moſt admirable repair.

The *Moſtyn* diſtrict begins at the weſtern end of the *Flint:* much of it is in very good order: part is very indifferent, owing to the impoveriſhed ſtate of the *Moſtyn* diſtrict, and to the inability of the poor inhabitants of the townſhip in which *Rhialltbill* lies, to repair that part, which is bad by nature. I propoſe a ſubſcription: you ſee my offer in the incloſed. We look up to the city of *Cheſter,* as both are engaged in a common cauſe.

The *Holywell* diſtrict is, excepting near *Halkin,* in excellent repair.

repair. The part complained of will be attended to at the next meeting at *Holywell*, at eleven o'clock on *Wednesday* the 8th of *February*. We fhall be happy to fee any gentlemen on the part of your city.

Excuse me if I remind the city of *Chefter*, the county, and alfo the county of *Flint*, that our importance is fuch, that our demand of a mail is a matter of right; not a petition for favor. How fuperior is the juftice of our claim to that of *Salop*, which had long fince its independent mail!

In refpect to my particular actings, I never will perfift in any thing that is wrong; nor defift from any thing that is right. Our clame for abolifhing the exemption from tolls is founded on common honefty. My feizing on the guàrd was the act of an attentive magiftrate, to prevent future murders. Two, if not three, had been committed: one near *Conwy*; another in *Anglefey*: befides the terror fpread along the whole road by the wanton conduct of the profligate guards. I brought the affair before our quarter-feffion; more to fet it in the true light than to punifh the offender. I was afperfed in your city; but the examination wiped away the dirty paragraph.

I am, Sir,

Your moft obedient humble fervant,

Thomas Pennant,

To the worfhipful the Mayor of Chefter.

To

To the Printer of the SHREWSBURY CHRONICLE,

SIR, *Downing, August 6, 1791.*

I REQUEST you to lay before the public the following advertisement, addressed by the commissioners of the *Mostyn* turnpike district, in order to avert in future the hardships several of the townships of the county of *Flint* labor under in the repairs of the roads. The advertisement itself relates to the greater part of the grievances. It was sent to the paper too late to inform the *English* circuits, but has been approved by the grand juries of *Cheshire*, *Denbighshire*, and *Flintshire*, at the Spring assizes, and by that of *Berkshire* and *Monmouthshire*, being the Autumn assizes. Let me here inform you, that, by indictments from the General Post-Office, fines to the amount of 1200 *l.* have been laid on the several townships lying in the course of the post-roads in the little county of *Flint*, many of which are very small, and labour under the greatest poverty. One in particular has a vast extent of road to repair, and only a few labourers, and four miserable teams to perform their statute labor. Under those circumstances, terrified with the prospect of ruin, they performed twenty-two days statute duty. The French *corvées*, now so reasonably abolished, were introduced on British ground, yet in vain; for a fine of 82 *l.* 10*s.* was imposed on the poor people. So little interested were they, and

S numbers

numbers of others of the *Welsh* townships, in the passage of the mail-coach, that possibly they do not receive a letter in a year; yet these townships must suffer equally with the most opulent and commercial towns.   Many of the roads were unexceptionably repaired; the rest were in sufficient repair for the uses of the farmer, for the uses of the gentlemen's carriages, and for the uses of the mail, before the late unguarded innovations.   We are, like the *Israelites*, required to make brick without straw. The means of repair are taken from us, and we are fined for not performing impossibilities.   A post-road is a national concern; that to a neighboring kingdom doubly so: and certainly that consideration should induce legislature to afford an aid in such cases in which it is found necessary; and if a road must be finished with finical perfection, the expence ought never to fall on those who are totally uninterested in it.   Justice can never require that the poor should keep pace with the innovations made for the benefit of commerce or luxury.   Much of the road-laws calls loudly for a reform: in all laws there should be a point of limitation.   The attention of the grand juries is requested at the ensuing assizes.   It is hoped that they will direct their representatives to make the mail-coaches liable to tolls.   We mean no injury to Mr. *Palmer:* let him, before the meeting of parlement, suggest any remedy for the evil, and we shall rest content.   They will certainly do away the great parlementary opprobrium of the act passed by their predecessors; which lessens a security granted on the faith of parlement.   And much more may be said on this subject; but the detail is reserved for another occasion; you may be again

troubled

troubled with my complaints, as well as some account of a township grievance, brought on it by those whose peculiar office it was to have guarded against the deceptions which imposed on their judgment, and brought on a most erroneous and disgraceful adjudication.

I am, Sir,

Your most obedient humble servant,

THOMAS PENNANT.

"GENERAL

" GENERAL TURNPIKE CONCERN.

1. " A T a meeting of the truſtees of the *Moſtyn* turnpike, held at the houſe of *Joſeph Roberts*, at the *Blue Bell*, on *Saturday*, *July* 30, 1791, the ſtate of the roads was taken into conſideration:

2. " WHEN it appeared, that parts of the coal-road were greatly out of repair; the trade in which was the original foundation of this turnpike.

3. " THAT the preſent annual tolls are very inadequate to remedy the evil.

4. " THAT the failure of the tolls does not ariſe from any decay of trade in the country, but from the exemption granted by parliament, by the 25th *Geo.* III. c. 57, to the mail-coaches from the payment of any tolls.

5. " THAT, by ſuch exemption, the common ſtage-coaches have been obliged to defiſt from travelling, by reaſon of the burthen they are ſingly to ſuſtain, and which the mail-coaches are freed from, and now in many places monopolize the buſineſs.

6. " THAT the *Moſtyn* diſtrict alone ſuffers a loſs of 40 *l.* a year, which is the intereſt of 800 *l.* the loſs of which prevents the truſtees from the repairing of road equal to the expenditure of ſuch a ſum.

7. " THAT the clauſe of exemption in favor of the mail-

coaches

coaches is highly detrimental to the credit of the tolls, and the security of the lenders, who had lent their money under the pledge of parliamentary faith.

8. " ORDERED, That the expediency of petitioning parliament on this subject be farther taken into consideration, and that these resolutions be published in the next *Chester* paper, as they are public concerns; every post-road, and its several creditors, being interested therein.

9. " THAT the sum of ten guineas be paid into the hands of the solicitor, towards the expences of the proposed bill, for repealing the exemption of tolls of the mail-coaches, and for subjecting them to tolls, in case such bill be brought into parliament: and that the commissioners of the several turnpike districts in *Great Britain* be invited to correspond, by their treasurers, on the subject, with *Samuel Small*, treasurer of the *Flint* and *Holywell* districts, and *John Lloyd*, assistant treasurer of that of *Mostyn*.

10. " THAT the thanks of the commissioners be given to the foremen and grand juries of the counties of *Cheshire*, *Denbighshire*, and *Flintshire*, for their liberal concurrence with the resolutions of the commissioners of the *Mostyn* district.

11. " THAT it is requested of the gentlemen of this county to attend at *Mold*, on *Saturday* the 9th of *April*, to give a sanction to this proposal, and to prepare one or more petitions, or to give necessary instruction to the representatives of the county and borough, &c. as may then be thought proper.

12. " AND, in order to give force to this reasonable clame

§   on

on parliament, it is recommended to the gentlemen of neighboring counties, who may attend the duty of their country on
the enfuing grand juries, to take the above into confideration,
and add their weight to the common caufe.

Signed, by order of the commiffioners,

" John Lloyd,

" *Affiftant Clerk and Treafurer*."

APPENDIX, N° 8:

MY LAST AND BEST WORK.

THE dangerous defigns of the *French* at this time became fo evident as to induce fome of my neighbors to call on me, and requeft that I would take the lead, and form an affociation for the defence of our religion, conftitution, and property, after the example of fome of the *Englifh* counties, cities, and towns; my zeal readily prompted me to comply with their requeft, and I drew up a requifition for a meeting in the following plain terms.

REQUISITION.

To the INHABITANTS and LAND-OWNERS of the Parifhes of *Holywell* and *Whitford*, in the County of *Flint*.

WE, whofe names are underwritten, do earneftly requeft you to meet us, on *Thurfday* the 20th inftant, at the *Antelope*, in *Holywell*, at the hour of Twelve, then and there to declare, and fubfcribe, our abhorrence of the treafonable and feditious practices of a few difaffected perfons, which are, to the beft of their power, helping the *French* to ruin our trade and

2   manufactures,

manufactures, to deftroy our religion, our laws, and our king, to leave the poor without any one able to give them bread, or to protect them from wrongs from great or fmall, and laftly, to bring confufion and deftruction upon this now happy, and flourifhing, kingdom.

I bawb fy'n caru Cymru*.

Holywell, Dec. 13, 1792.

JOHN WHITTAKER	THOMAS PENNANT
JAMES SHELDON	J. ELLIS MOSTYN.
JOHN ELLIS SUTTON	JOHN LLOYD, clerk
BELL GRAHME	THO. EDWARDS, *Saeth aelwyd*
REV. PHILIP JONES	CHRISTOPHER SMALLEY
WILLIAM CHAMBERS, grocer	ROBERT HUGHES
JAMES POTTS, publican	EDWARD HUGHES
JOHN LLOYD, farmer	WM. BRAMWELL, maltfter
JOSEPH ROBERTS, publican	D. DONBAVAND, *Greenfield.*
SAMUEL WILLIAMSON	

* To all who love WALES.

This

This ADVERTISEMENT produced the following

A S S O C I A T I O N.

At a MEETING of the INHABITANTS of the Parishes of

Holywell,	*Caerwys,*
Whitford,	*Newmarket,*
Northop,	*Llanhafa,*
Flint,	*Saint Afaph,*
Halkin,	*Rhuddlan,*
Kilken,	*Meliden,*
Skeiviog,	*Diferth,*
Nannerch,	*Cwm,*

IN THE COUNTY OF FLINT,

Held at the *Antelope,* in the Town of *Holywell,* on *Thurfday* the 20th day of *December,* 1792;

Refolved unanimoufly,

THAT it is the opinion of this meeting, that affociations of all perfons enjoying the unexampled benefits of the happy and envied conftitution of *Great-Britain,* are at this time highly expedient and neceffary, to affift in preferving the eftablifhed liberties and growing profperity of our country.

We do therefore affociate ourfelves ;—and do profefs and declare our unalienable attachment to the Conftitution, our firm and inviolable allegiance to our gracious Sovereign, under whofe mild and beneficent reign we poffefs all the advantages of good

T

government;

government; our obedience to the laws, and our anxious wifhes for peace and good order in fociety, which it is our determined refolution to ufe all our exertions to preferve; and we do exprefs our abhorrence of every attempt made to deprive us of the invaluable bleffings we now enjoy.

Thus affociated, we feel it our duty to point out, and we requeft all orders of men in this country to reflect on, the ineftimable benefits of our excellent conftitution.

We are governed by known laws, that are juft and equal, and refpect not perfons; they alike reftrain oppreffion and curb licentioufnefs : *The higheft* (as hath been well obferved) *are within their reach, and the loweft have their full protection.*

All the arts, farming, manufactures, trade, and every employment and labour of man, are encouraged, and flourifh beyond any thing known in any former period, or in any country; every man poffeffes in fecurity the fruit of his labour. Talents and induftry are fure of fuccefs, and may, as we daily fee, rife to wealth and honor.

We enjoy, and have long enjoyed, the perfection of civil liberty in our perfons, our property, and our honeft opinions : and it is the glory of *Britain,* that of all the nations of *Europe—HERE ONLY ALL MEN ARE FREE.*

It is then our duty, and we folemnly pledge ourfelves, collectively and individually, to ufe our utmoft endeavors to preferve thefe invaluable bleffings, by a firm and zealous attachment to our King and Conftitution, a ready and ftrenuous fupport of the magiftracy, and the moft active and unremitted vigilance to fupprefs and prevent all tumult, diforder, and feditious meetings and publications.

Refolved,

Resolved, That the thanks of this meeting be given to THO-
MAS PENNANT, Esq. chairman, for his activity and zeal in promoting this business, and his ready acceptance of the chair.

Resolved, That the thanks of this meeting be given to EDWARD
JONES, Esq. of *Wepre-hall*, for his attention in drawing up the
resolutions of this meeting, above recited.

Resolved, That a committee be formed of this Association,
consisting of the following gentlemen;

THOMAS PENNANT, Esq. Chairman;

SIR ROGER MOSTYN, Bart. M. P.
SIR EDWARD LLOYD, Bart.
WATKIN WILLIAMS, Esq. M. P.
REV. THE DEAN OF ST. ASAPH,
ROBERT HUGHES, Esq.
EDW. MORGAN, Esq.
THO. WILLIAMS, Esq.
EDWARD JONES, Esq.
MR. DANIEL DONBAVAND,
THO. TOTTY, Esq.
CHRISTOPHER SMALLEY, Esq.
JOHN WHITTAKER, Esq.
JOHN ELLIS MOSTYN, Esq.
SAMUEL SMALL, Esq.
HUGH HUMPHREYS, Esq.
WM. ALLEN, Esq.
REV. JOHN LLOYD, *Holywell*,
REV. PHILIP JONES,
THOMAS THOMAS, Esq.

REV. EDW. HUGHES, *Greenfield*,
REV. JOHN POTTER,
PAUL PANTON, Esq.
DAVID PENNANT, Esq.
REV. JOHN LLOYD, *Caerwys*,
MR. FRANCIS SMEDLEY,
REV. THO. HUGHES, *Bagillt*,
MR. SAMUEL DAVIES, grocer
MR. THOMAS THORESBY,
MR. SAMUEL WILLIAMSON,
JOHN DOUGLAS, Esq.
JOHN LLOYD, Gent.
JOHN ELLIS SUTTON, Gent.
REV. HENRY PARRY,
MR. WILLIAM CHAMBERS,
MR. THOMAS SIMON,
MR. BELL GRAHME,
REV. JOS. TYRER.

Resolved, That JOHN ELLIS SUTTON be appointed secretary to
this committee.

T 2

Resolved,

Refolved, That ten of the perfons above mentioned may form a committee.

Refolved, That a committee be held on every *Saturday,* till it is forbidden; and that the firft be held on *Saturday* the 5th of *January,* at the hour of eleven, at the *Antelope,* in *Holywell.*

Refolved, That the clergy of the feveral affociated parifhes be requefted to return the books to the fecretary, on or before *January* the 5th, being the firft committee.

Refolved, That any other parifh in *Flintfhire,* which may happen to affociate, be requefted to tranfmit to the fecretary notice of fuch affociation, that, if needful, they may hereafter correfpond together.

Refolved, That the proceedings of this day be publifhed in *Adams'*s Weekly Courant; and that EDMUND MONK be printer to this affociation.

THOMAS PENNANT, Chairman.

A BOOK for receiving the fignatures of the feveral parifhes, was fent to each, with the above refolutions, tranflated into *Welfh,* prefixed, and alfo a copy of Mr. Juftice *Afhurft'*s fpeech given in the fame language, for the benefit of thofe who did not underftand *Englifh;* and thefe books were figned by an incredible number of people.

COUNTY

COUNTY BOUNTIES

FOR SEAMEN.

———————

FLINTSHIRE.

Holywell, Feb. 2, 1793.

WE, whofe names are underwritten, members of the committee of the fixteen affociated parifhes in *Flintfhire*, this
day affembled, do hereby offer two guineas (over and above all
other bounties) to each of the firft twenty Able Seamen, natives
of *Flintfhire*, and one guinea apiece to each of the firft twenty
Ordinary Seamen, or Landmen, natives of the fame county, who
are willing to enter into his majefty's fervice, to defend their
religion, their king, their wives, children, or friends, from a moft
wicked and barbarous enemy.

ANY brave fellow, fo inclined, is defired to apply to Mr.
John Ellis Sutton, fecretary of the committee, at *Holywell*, who

will

will inform him of other particulars, and give him a recommendation to his majesty's regulating captain at *Liverpool*.

THIS to continue in force for three months.

				£.
ROGER MOSTYN	—		—	42
THOMAS PENNANT	—	—	—	21
WILLIAM DAVIES SHIPLEY		—	—	21
WATKIN WILLIAMS	—		—	21
HOPE WYNNE EYTON, for five able seamen.				
LEWIS ST. ASAPH	—	—	—	21

and more, if required.

ANY public-spirited *Flintshire* men, willing to encourage this
undertaking in the smallest degree, are requested to send in their
names to the chairman, as subscribers to one or more Able Seamen, or Ordinary Seamen, as may suit their inclination or con-
veniency.

THIS was the first county-bounty which had been offered.
The example was instantly followed in *Chester*, and four places
in *North Wales*. The committee of the sixteen parishes were
immediately honored with the unsolicited thanks of the Lords
of the Admiralty.

THE instances of the public spirit of the Ladies of *Flintshire*
must not be passed over in silence.

To

To the EDITOR of ADAMS'S COURANT.

SIR,

YOU will be pleafed to infert in your next paper the following letter, worthy of a CHARLOTTE DE LA TREMOUILLE*.
It is not only a tribute due to the lady's public fpirit, but may
prove an incentive to others to follow an example worthy of the
imitation of every good man.

" To the Chairman of the Committee of the Sixteen affociated
Parifhes in FLINTSHIRE.

" DEAR SIR,   *Wrexham, Feb.* 15, 1793.

" I feel fo much pleafed with the fpirited exertions of yourfelf
and the other *Flintfhire* gentlemen, expreffed in the advertifement in *Monk*'s laft paper, that I muft beg you to accept of
the inclofed, to be applied to the fame purpofe; and, as it is a
duty that every individual owes to that conftitution that has
protected their life and property, to do their utmoft to fupport it
at this awful period, if you want my further affiftance, you may
command the fame fum whenever you chufe to call for it.

" I am, dear Sir,

" Your affectionate kinfwoman,

" MARY PULESTON."

* Countefs of Derby, in the reign of Charles I.

At

At a Meeting of the **COMMITTEE** of the
HOLYWELL ASSOCIATION,
Held 16th *February* 1793, at the *Antelope*, in *Holywell*,
IT WAS ORDERED,

THAT public thanks be given to Mrs. PULESTON, for her above fpirited donation; and that her letter be printed in *Adams*'s next Courant.

T. PENNANT, Chairman.

Other Contributors fince February 6th.

	£.	s.	d.
Mrs. PULESTON of *Gwyfaney*	10	10	0
And an offer of the like fum, if required.			
Mrs. EVANS, *Holywell*	2	2	0
Mr. *Lewis Hughes St. Afaph*	3	3	0
Mr. *John Davies* of Gop	1	1	0
The Rev. *Edward Hughes* of *Kinmael*	10	10	0
Thomas S. Chamneys, Efq.	10	10	0
and more, if required.			

F I N I S.

For EU product safety concerns, contact us at Calle de José Abascal, 56–1°,
28003 Madrid, Spain or eugpsr@cambridge.org.

www.ingramcontent.com/pod-product-compliance
Ingram Content Group UK Ltd.
Pitfield, Milton Keynes, MK11 3LW, UK
UKHW030902150625
459647UK00021B/2667